IGNACE SCHOPS

SAVED BY THE TREE FROG

A BRIGHT FUTURE FOR MANKIND AND NATURE

Lannoo
Campus

This book was originally published as *Gered door de boomkikker.
De grote toekomst van mens en natuur*, LannooCampus Publishers, 2022.

D/2023/45/371 – ISBN 978 94 014 9734 3 – NUR 740, 940

COVER DESIGN Adept vormgeving
PAGE DESIGN LetterLust | Stefaan Verboven
TYPESETTING Keppie & Keppie
EDITING Koos de Wilt
TRANSLATION Lynn Butler

LannooCampus Publishers is a subsidiary of Lannoo Publishers,
the book and multimedia division of Lannoo Publishers nv.

LannooCampus Publishers
Vaartkom 41 bus 01.02   Postbus 23202
3000 Leuven   1100 DS Amsterdam
Belgium   The Netherlands

www.lannoocampus.com

International praise
for Ignace Schops's work

'To Ignace: Because of the work that you and
your team have done, bringing nature to people,
reconnecting nature with nature and with people,
and involving business and involving government
policy, so that you've proved with all your efforts,
you and your team, that preserving nature is
not only good for the natural world and wildlife,
but for us as well. We need that connection with
nature. We are part of the natural word, and
we depend on it.'

'I guess, Ignace, that you are one of those
indomitable spirits, because during all these
efforts to create the national parks, I know
you've met many obstacles but you've stuck
with it, and you won through, and proved
that it can be done.'

DAME JANE GOODALL
British primatologist and anthropologist

'Had a great conversation with Ignace Schops
on the origins of climate reality and personal
experiences as Climate Reality Leaders.
Keep up the great work as you continue to
#LeadOnClimate!'

AL GORE
Former Vice President of the United States of America,
winner of the Nobel Peace Prize, author of *An Inconvenient Truth*

'Dear Ignace: never give up.'

SIR DAVID ATTENBOROUGH
British broadcaster, biologist,
natural historian and author

Table of contents

Chapter 2

BIODIVERSITY, CLIMATE AND AGRICULTURE SOLUTIONS

What exactly are we talking about? 71

Chapter 3

TOWARDS A DIFFERENT ECONOMIC MODEL

The (Re)connection Model: inspiration for a pact between ecology and economics 125

Chapter 4

WHAT CAN WE DO?

Give nature back its rights 167

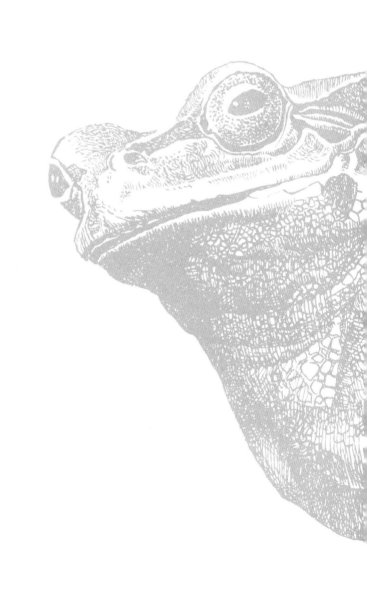

"I am because we are."

– Ubuntu philosophy

"Faith is the bird that feels
the light and sings when
the dawn is still dark."

– Rabindranath Tagore

ECONOMY VERSUS ECOLOGY?

How nature is helping us save the climate,
biodiversity and our economy

Nothing tastes as intense as a memory. It was April 1991 when – as a passionate conservationist – I stood in the lake's water in my waders, face to face with a tiny grass-green tree frog. Its toes were adorned with characteristic suction cup-like adhesive pads, and it had a distinctive dark stripe that seemed to emerge from its nose, dash across its back and run under its belly like a sharp line dividing the frog in two. Tree frogs are always a striking and unusual sight, but especially during mating season when hundreds of male tree frogs drift together in a giant flotilla. They call out in unison, producing a hellish and staccato barrage of sound that lures females from miles away to mate.

This special experience seemed more powerful than usual on that distant April day. Soon the racket of the males that had permeated the air gave way to a catchy and gripping concert of rhythmic 'squawking' sounds. I remember, as if it were yesterday, my surprise that the tree frog floating closest to me did not jump away but looked me straight in the eye while continuing to croak loudly. It was as if he wanted to tell me something, or to be precise, to shout something at me. Even though I did not understand the tree frog's message, I immediately understood its metaphorical meaning: let me live and stop destroying nature. As remarkable as it may seem, that small frog offered me a vision that has never left me. And his message did not end there. Still the frog did not jump away but kept croaking loudly in my direction: do something!

I was transfixed by an inspiration of almost magical dimensions. On that day it became crystal clear to me that our disposable economy is rapidly undoing millions of years of evolution. The importance of diversity, of the fact that our environment is an interdependent network, and that we are dependent upon that network, became self-evident to me. Also, that the environment holds within it the seeds for the future of humanity and nature, that we are, in fact, one and the same. I was awakened to the reality that every animal, every life form has a right to exist, and has a place and purpose in a wider ecosystem.

If we recognise and accept our interdependence and demonstrate this in our behaviour and in the economy, then we can recognise our own potential. The logical and critical conclusion is that we must invest in nature because nature is precisely what keeps us alive. We have reached a crucial point of departure in our evolution, one which demands that we discard our self-centred human perspectives and reconnect with nature and all its life forms. As a society, and as individuals, we bear a crushing responsibility. It is we who determine the value of a tree frog's life. It is we who decide if the tree frogs should live at all. We decide. We human beings are an inseparable part of nature. We are nature. From the moment we really start understanding this, we will start doing something about it. To save the tree frog is to save ourselves. It is as simple as that.

For now, we are on an uncertain track. Our current economic model and our actions show that we embrace the disconcerting notion of the eternal burning lamp and pretend that doing this is the most natural thing in the world. The error in our thinking is illustrated by the following story of a lightbulb in California that demonstrates in a surprising manner how our economy works.

In 1901 an old paraffin lantern at a fire station in the small town of Livermore, California was replaced by a light bulb manufactured by the Shelby Electric Company. A fireman switched on the light, unaware of the miraculous phenomenon he had started. That switch was turned on more than 120 years ago, but that same bulb has burnt ever since. In truth, it was turned off for a very short time when the fire station was relocated, but that does not detract from this remarkable lighting achievement. No one could have guessed that a bulb could burn for that long. The town has become world-famous for the bulb and promotes itself as: 'Livermore, California's Centennial Light. Home of the world's longest burning light bulb.' A webcam allows us to watch the bulb burning online at www.centennialbulb. org. As extraordinary as this story is, indirectly this lamp has cast a long shadow over our relentless hunger for more. This perspective demands our attention.

From landfill to circular vision

Thomas Edison's invention of the light bulb literally brought light into the darkness. But the history of its commercialisation exemplifies how we have come to organise our western economy. So, what happened? Shortly after its invention, clever engineers figured out how to improve the quality and performance of light bulbs. Spurred on by the mechanisation of production, light bulbs could be made in large numbers relatively quickly. A bulb that could glow for a very long time would be attractive to consumers. By the early twentieth century, light bulb design had been perfected to the degree that bulbs could burn for 2500 hours! And as we now know, light bulbs that lasted more than a century could be produced.

Companies like Philips, Osram, and General Electric were keen to cement their stake in the future of artificial lighting. For this reason, *Phoebus SA Compagnie Industrielle pour le Développement de l'Éclairage*, later called the Phoebus cartel, was formed in 1925. Their aim was to improve inter-corporate cooperation between bulb manufacturers, exchange patents and increase the quality of lighting. The fact that all lamps had the same screw thread – incidentally, like the light bulb, also one of Edison's inventions – was agreed through the Phoebus cartel. So far so good. But there was great concern about the extraordinary performance of light bulbs. The product was too durable, too good in other words. The global cartel felt that continued improvements to light bulbs was 'a bad business model' because it meant they could sell far fewer bulbs. They decided the following: to sell more lamps, sell more bulbs and make more profit, they would reduce the maximum allowed performance per bulb from 2,500 light hours to a maximum of 1,000 light hours, a drop of 60 per cent. All new light bulb models would henceforth be tested in a laboratory in Basel, Switzerland. Manufacturers who produced bulbs that exceeded this rating were punished with a fine that increased as a function of length of time the bulbs burned beyond 1,000 light hours. What the Phoebus cartel decided was out of order, you might think, but it was a model for the way we have organised our western disposable economy. In other words, we operate under an economic model driven only by profit, with no regard for the finite nature of raw materials and no acknowledgement of its impact on nature and society. This story is the forerunner of today's business credo, best summarised as: new means almost broken, designed to break down quickly, to quickly become waste, in essence new means designed for landfill.

Designing products to be destined for landfill can be considered literally as a universally valid business model. Have we any idea of the impact of our Western lifestyle over the last 50 years? We often buy things we don't need, with money we don't have, and an environmental impact we don't want. We fly to Rome or Barcelona without wondering how this could be made possible for a 16 euro return ticket. We visit the zoo, excited to see the ring-tailed lemurs displayed in a fake jungle, without a thought about where these magnificent creatures come from and the fate of their wild relatives in the real jungle of Madagascar. We have adopted a lifestyle that has lost any connection with nature.

We are like frogs in a cooking pot that is heated little by little, realising too late that they are being cooked. Meanwhile, we are preoccupied with trivialities. Why do we get so upset at the death of Princess Diana or Diego Maradona, yet we think nothing of the death of Lonesome George, the last endemic Pinta tortoise in the Galápagos Islands, and the threat to the natural environment that is home to billions of people? Why is it, after all, that we are distressed by the COVID pandemic or the dioxin crisis but not about the loss of biodiversity and climate change? We expect the fire brigade will put out every blaze and follow up to prevent possible flare-ups, but we seem resigned to our failure to act on the much more dangerous consequences of climate change and the destruction of natural ecosystems. We know we are heading for a fire that no fire brigade can withstand if we do not try to prevent and put out the first fires now. And yet very little is happening ...

In this book, I try to make it clear that nature with all its biodiversity must again be put first and lead our thinking and our personal, political and economic actions. In the first chapter, I show that we simply have no choice and must take immediate action. The simple message is: there will be no business on a dead planet. I also show that taking action requires leadership of the calibre we had when we decided to set foot on the moon within ten years, only this time we need a leadership to decide to keep human life possible on earth: in other words, from a Moonshot to an Earthshot.

In Chapter 2, I try to shed light on the noise surrounding issues like biodiversity and climate problems and try to clarify exactly what we are talking about. What is the uncomfortable, unambiguous and clear truth about the state of our nature, about our chances of survival and about our possibilities? What exactly are the uncomfortable facts that scientists agree on? In Chapter 3, I explain how we can define a process to save our planet, collaborating globally, but also on an individual level. I address how we can continue to earn a living while securing the basis of our existence: nature. I do this using the so-called (Re)connection Model, a model I have developed over the years with the brightest minds and with the decisive support of the Regionaal Landschap Kempen, a nature reserve in Maasland, Belgium. I will also introduce you to a new world and new financing models. I show how financing logic can be changed by putting the planet on the stock market and keeping climate investments off budget, how we can create a booster for nature with a Green Tax Shelter and the voluntary carbon market. I talk about how the value of nature can be included in cost analysis and explain how the (Re)connection Model can serve as an inspiration of how we can save nature on the one hand and find a way to make our society more beautiful on the other. I will describe a new and logical way of assigning value that takes into account how humans have taken most of their existence for granted, which is extraordinarily similar to how scientists see the future. In Chapter 4, I talk about the rights of nature as a successor to the rights we have acquired as humans: a game-changer in our approach to saving biodiversity and our climate.

Overall, my objective for this book is to show that we need not hang our heads, because the control of our relationship with nature is within our zone of control both locally and globally. I will show readers how an old mining region has been developed into a genuine national park, the Hoge Kempen National Park in Belgium, where nature has been saved and people have regained a dignified perspective, decades after so many of their family members in the same area had lost their jobs in the closing of the Belgian coal mining industry. Nature has been given its own space there, while outside the park guests are welcomed and pampered by proud residents of the region. In addition, I show readers that no matter how big the challenges around climate change and biodiversity are, we must push forward now. 'The most dangerous worldview is the worldview of those who have not viewed the world,' said the recently deceased Edward O. Wilson, renowned worldwide for his contributions in the fields of biodiversity and biogeography. We need to look more openly, broadly and honestly at the world around us. No more thinking in terms of zero sum, but in terms of win-win.

We need to look more openly, broadly and honestly at the world around us. No more thinking in terms of zero sum, but in terms of win-win.

No more looking only at the monkey sitting on the top of the rock, but also at all those other animals and micro-organisms that shape nature. Not just thinking in terms of struggle, but also in terms of working together, exactly as nature presents itself to us.

But first let me tell you a little story to illustrate the situation we are in now. Imagine that it is about 15 years ago you have booked a city trip to Barcelona. You pack and arrive at the airport two hours before your flight as requested, your passport is checked, and you pass through security with flying colours. You have ample time to dream about the delightful prospect of a steel-blue sky and the warm rays of the Spanish sun on your face. You are startled by the sound of a friendly female voice on the public address system: 'Dear passengers travelling to Barcelona, we are about to commence boarding. Please have your passport and boarding pass ready.' Finally! Everyone jumps up and rushes to the gate, lining up for a final security check before boarding the plane. But another announcement is made: 'Dear passengers travelling to Barcelona. We would like to draw your attention to the fact that the plane is missing six parts and twelve screws. Please board at your own risk. Have a nice trip!' So, what do you do? Board or not? What do you do when the risk of danger is so immediate and obvious to everyone? Right. You curse and rant and wonder how such a thing could be possible. You consider legal action. You cannot understand how the government could allow such irresponsible behaviour. Indignant and angry, you return home. And even now, fifteen years later, you still tell the story to your children and grandchildren: 'If I had boarded that plane, I would not be here now.' At the time, you had the knowledge you needed to make the right decision. You may have realised by now that this little story is analogous to where we are today. This story is even more real and current than we might realise. Try thinking of our planet, with all its forms of life, as an immense plane, like one big living machine with each species functioning as an essential part. You realise that just one cog in a clock will stop your watch from keeping time, that one missing connection in a microchip will prevent your laptop from starting. How many cogs or microchips do we need to keep our unique and well-tuned living engine functioning forever? If you knew that every day many forms of life would vanish, never to return, how would you react? Indifferent? Wait-and-see? Or not? The good news is that there is a way out...

Lessons from the pandemic

As I write this, I am sitting in 'diversity', one of the three think boxes in LABIOMISTA, the home base of my good friend and world renowned artist Koen Vanmechelen. LABIOMISTA – literally meaning 'mix of life' – is an evolving work of art on the foundations of the former mine and zoo of Zwartberg in the Belgian city of Genk. Koen's work is based on cultural and biological diversity and he is one of the most versatile thinkers I know. The coronavirus is still not completely off our radars yet. Meanwhile, despite the turmoil and all the grief, the pandemic has made us a lot wiser. Yes, now that it is over or more or less over, we have quickly relapsed into our old habits. But we still learned something about equality. Even if the future sometimes seems hopeless, maybe now is the time for connection and introspection. This pandemic is a warning, a wake-up call. No matter how lost we sometimes feel these days, perhaps the time has come to think deeply and reflect on who we are, how we relate to our human and non-human surroundings far away and nearby. Perhaps the pandemic can help us gain that insight? Can we build a nature-rich, sustainable and warm society? Will we succeed in learning to appreciate again the comfort, power and value of everyday life? Few of us thought that what is happening today, right before our eyes, could ever be possible. The pandemic is proof that sound decisions can be made based on scientific insights from experts and scientists. In record time, we not only developed a coronavirus vaccine, but we also confirmed its safety and efficacy at lightning speed. We proved capable of rapid changes in our behaviour to live and survive. We kept our distance and even today many continue to wear mouth masks to protect others. Most of us have learned to see things from the perspective of a group over that of the individual. We have reawakened to the fact that we get much further as a society than as individuals. We also sometimes marvel at the incredible selfishness that the corona crisis has revealed in a minority of people. Above all, the pandemic has taught us that – when it comes down to it – cost is not an obstacle. We suddenly have the guts and decisiveness to find the billions of euros when it is necessary.

We seem to be moving back towards a more inclusive system where we realise that we can only make something good out of bad situations when we work together. In doing so, we can learn from the traditional and age-old South African Ubuntu philosophy: 'I am because we are'. This means that only by working together can we survive as a community. Archbishop Desmond Tutu, who died in December 2021, described that philosophy in 1999 as follows: 'A person with Ubuntu is open to and accessible to others, devotes himself or herself to others, does not feel threatened by the ability of others because he or she draws enough self-confidence from the knowledge that he or she is part of a greater whole, and cringes when others are humiliated or when others are tortured or oppressed.' This may sound a bit edifying, but it touches on the world we face more and more every day. There is no more room for selfish individual behaviour. A world where climate issues are already banging loudly on our doors and where we hear the unsettling rumble of a tsunami in the background, of the collapse of our world's biodiversity. A world we can only save together. The answers are there for the taking and it all starts with simply thinking differently and more honestly about the world we live in.

From Paris to your own backyard

Our planet is currently in an existential state of emergency, sending out alarm signals that are not obvious to everyone and do not always sound convincing. At the last climate summit before the publication of this book, in Sharm-el-Sheikh in Egypt, world leaders looked each other in the eye for the umpteenth time. Speakers from countries that might survive the next few decades took the floor, but also those from countries that are first in line to suffer from the effects of the damage we have caused to the environment. Many millions of people cannot afford or do not have the luxury to ignore the risks even for a moment, while others do not feel the need. Yet we will all suffer the disastrous consequences if we do not take action. As President Obama said in 2014, 'We are the first generation to feel the impact of climate change and the last generation that can do something about it.' Following the latest synthesis report (2023) of the Intergovernmental Panel on Climate Change (IPCC), United Nations Secretary-General António Guterres warned: 'We are on a highway to climate hell with our foot still on the accelerator'. The next decade is extremely important. Do we succeed in giving the tree frog – nature – back its rightful place and can we change the climate before the climate will change us? Can we find a sustainable balance that respects both people and nature? Can we save ourselves, can we let the tree frog help us?

In a world where many feel lonely, but where just about everything and everyone seems to be digitally connected, finding transformative solutions is extremely complex and confounded by an ever-changing context. But just because something seems hopeless or complex doesn't mean we do not have a damned duty to find a way out. I am genuinely outraged by the way we treat our Mother Earth, how we as humans saw off the branch on which we ourselves sit. I want to turn that indignation not just into anger and negative energy but use it as a source of renewable energy. Into positive energy and strength that shows we can actually get the job done together, through rock-solid confidence, by thinking clearly, by turning our thinking around, by making choices and by taking effective action. Locally and globally. It really can be done.

I wrote this book because I believe that in the problem lies the solution. That the systemic and sustainable transition is in the connection, rather than in the opposition. Sustainable change pays off better in cooperation than in opposition. For too long have we deluded ourselves that everything is a battle of all against all and that only a few of us get to sit atop the monkey rock. Too seldom have we noticed that nature is not just a battle of survival of the fittest, but that it is also a continuous chain of cooperation, of adapting to each other and exchanging to survive, together.

Not long ago, we were surprised by the scientific insight that trees actually communicate with each other, that their roots cooperate with fungi that in turn cooperate with roots of other trees. A great insight that makes us realise that we need to connect with each other and with nature. Everything is connected to everything and very often the battle to be won has been a battle we have fought together. In this sense, economics and ecology need not be enemies of each other, just as agriculture need not be an opponent of nature. More than that, they can – and should – become each other's allies. While the systemic transformation, the reversal, the journey towards a sustainable planet and society is complex, it starts from a strong belief that change is possible and that our relationship with nature plays an existential role in this.

Biodiversity and climate are central to this book, along with the rock-solid belief that sustainable change must and still can be done. We just must choose that it can. Martin Luther King never started his speeches with 'I have a nightmare'. He had a dream that still inspires and drives many millions of people to make a better world. Let us dream of a sustainable and nature-rich future: for the tree frog, for ourselves and for our children. And above all, let us make those dreams come true together. We must dare to believe that it can be done. And if you don't believe in it (yet), I want to convince you with this book and make you happy against your will.

Chapter 1

"Dream the dreams
that have never been dreamt."

– David Bower

NO BUSINESS ON A DEAD PLANET

The hard truth about economics, nature and society,
and the unique opportunity of Earthshot thinking

We have developed a skewed relationship with nature. How has this happened? Science has taught us about the perilous state of our environment. Why is it that we do not act on this knowledge? This chapter will explore these questions. I present everything we know about how careless we are with nature; how we have been guided solely by an economic narrative and why we can no longer afford to be led only by our economic desires.

A quote from the actor David Bower fits this situation perfectly: 'Dream the dreams that have never been dreamt.' We simply must live a dream we have never dreamt before to pull off what is so obviously needed – to do everything we can to save this planet. We must act on the stark reality that there is no business, no economy on a dead planet, that it is not possible to discuss how to keep global industries intact and ensure that we regain biodiversity and save our climate. Things must and will have to change. So, it is time to show that we humans can achieve an extraordinary feat in a short time, an accomplishment that will save us all. A joint act of world leaders and people like you and me.

Why do we think the way we do about nature?

A lot is going wrong with biodiversity and the climate on our planet. Many businesses see it as in their interest to create confusion around this. Our common interests are being shamefully trampled on to secure short-term profits for those who doubt the scientific evidence.

Vision and decisiveness are needed to stop serving the financial interests of a few and make it possible to choose what to do to insure our
common survival on this planet. We need the calibre of leadership and
decisiveness we had some 60 years ago when we decided to set foot
on the moon within 10 years. We have increased our understanding
of what nature is and how we relate to it. We already have all the
information we need to decide to save the planet and to save ourselves.

Let me take you through the history of how we view nature and
how our views have evolved over time.

During much of our history we did not think of nature as a thing
of beauty as we do today, enhanced by nature films and accompanied by glorious music. As recently as a few hundred years ago we
saw nature as a monster that we had to fight against. From the 13th
century onwards when explorers like Marco Polo weighed anchor
and sailed across the seas into the wide world in wooden ships, those
sailing heroes became intimately aware of the beautiful but sometimes
treacherous aspects of their surroundings and the forces of nature.

Becoming seasick on one of those ships was trivial compared to
the other things that could happen to the explorers. The discovery
of odd creatures and strange-looking people speaking unintelligible
languages led to many extraordinary but also bloody and degrading
encounters, exploitation and slavery. This period could be characterised as a struggle of people against people, of the alleged 'civilised
versus savages', against a background struggle of man versus an unpre-
dictable and horrific natural world that had to be overcome.

Meeting and confronting unfamiliar people, animals, environments and ecosystems frequently resulted in unprecedented, painful
and even deadly infections. The disappearance of entire societies in
South America was in part due to the arrival of Spanish explorers who
carried contagious diseases as well as impressive weapons. Ancient
civilisations like the Incas fell victim to diseases like smallpox that
travelled with the Spanish ships. Without any visible cause or explanation, native people fell seriously ill, and often died.

Human populations have been repeatedly decimated by what initially seemed inexplicable causes that were later found to be the work
of viruses and bacteria. These strange, invisible primal forces of nature

were historically seen as supernatural and dangerous adversaries that humans were not equipped to counter.

Wherever the first adventurers landed, they were surrounded by a mighty, untouched and capricious wilderness with unfamiliar species of plants and animals around every corner. Interest in these strange-looking species grew. From the 16th century onwards, grand enterprises were set up to discover the richness and ingenuity of nature up close; even if it meant shooting the birds and other animals from the trees to examine them in detail. It was in that period that scientists began to question the Biblical creation story and the Cartesian worldview that places humans above all other life forms. In the early nineteenth century, for instance, it occurred to the renowned and itinerant German scientist Alexander von Humboldt that everything in nature was connected to everything else; an innovative view of nature that has gently become commonplace only in our time. Fortunately for the next generation of scientists the prescient von Humboldt recorded his knowledge and observations in five volumes that he named *Cosmos*, published over the years 1845-1862. The books were eagerly anticipated and read and resulted in von Humboldt in later days to be dubbed the *inventor of nature*.

From that point on, knowledge about nature grew at an ever-faster pace. Scientists were inspired by the recorded knowledge of their predecessors, passed on in letters exchanged between the scientific geniuses of the time, and based on their own progressive and often empirical research. Several scientists established that all species do not occur everywhere, and that some species prefer specific habitats and special conditions. This was a revolutionary idea that arose less than 200 years ago. The imaginations of a few perceptive researchers were triggered by the small differences they noticed between seemingly similar species. Suddenly, new insights and discoveries came at lightning speed. Naturalists began to race in their search for the origins of life, eager to discover the mechanisms behind the emergence of the species.

The answer would soon arrive. Gentleman naturalist Charles Darwin sailed with the Beagle out of Plymouth Sound in 1831, on a five-year voyage of exploration around the coast of South America. The observations he recorded on the trip resulted in his masterpiece *On the Origin of Species*, published in 1859, in which he described with his theory of evolution that all life on earth has a common ancestor, and that natural and sexual selection are the main mechanisms for the evolution of species; an insight that was unthinkable just a few generations earlier.

Darwin's theory was that evolution never stops, that it is a continuum, a mesh of mutual interactions. He proposed that through natural selection the strongest and most adapted species survive, but that survival can also be achieved through communal cooperation. The insights of perhaps the greatest scientist of all time opened our minds and taught us to appreciate the magnificence of nature, how in nature everything is interconnected with everything else, nature is resilient, and that nature constantly manages to adapt to changes in local environments.

Darwin's work encouraged admiration for nature's incredible resilience and resourcefulness. Yet we failed to abandon our arrogant attitude towards nature, and we ignored nature's wisdom. Fuelled by the Industrial Revolution in the second half of the eighteenth century, prosperity rose visibly in the western world and the population grew exponentially. Meanwhile, little by little, we came to be aware that nature's patience and resilience are not infinite. The riches of the natural world have been a lifeline to help millions escape from abject poverty. Yet it has begun to dawn on us that eventually there will be a price to be paid, that nature is not ours for free, forever.

In the 20th century, the idea began to emerge that we could not continue to enrich ourselves indefinitely at the expense of nature. An awareness about the viability of our planet has been sparked by the frightening realisation that nature's resilience is finite.

The first truly powerful wake up call to bring concerns about the future of the world into the limelight was the establishment of the Club of Rome in 1968. Its members were European scientists led by Italian industrialist Aurelio Pecci and Scottish scientist Alexander King. The club published a landmark report *Limits to Growth: A Global Challenge*, in 1972. The report examined environment effects that would result from projected levels of world population growth, industrialisation, pollution, food production and depletion of natural resources. The results were shocking and proved that *business as usual* – just carrying on – would lead to the destruction of our natural ecosystems and resources.

The Club of Rome report was based on a scientific analysis of available data from 1900 through 1970. It was released exactly 100 years after Yellowstone National Park was established in the US. We could no longer maintain that we were on the right track simply by opening national parks. On the contrary, the more parks there are the more easily we are lulled into believing that we can abuse nature without consequence.

Later research made it even more clear that with unbridled economic growth the stability of our climate will be thrown out of balance. Limiting economic growth was determined to be the only option to stay in balance and live within the limits of our planet. Voilà, the word was out. There has yet to be a rigorous response. The Club of Rome report has been updated several times and its conclusions remain largely valid to this day. There are limits to growth. No doubt about it.

The messages in the Club of Rome report gave its members entry to the highest political circles. Awareness about nature and environmental issues received a huge boost with the establishment of the United Nations Environment Programme (UNEP), founded by Canadian business leader and philanthropist Maurice Strong in 1972. All of today's climate, nature and sustainability policies have their origins in UNEP. From then on, membership in nature and environmental movements grew and the influence of these groups gained in importance. In short, since 1972 we really no longer ignore the truth that we humans are ruining our environment. Now that everyone had become aware of the disastrous consequences of our – mainly western – way of life, it was high time for change. Or was it?

Since 1972, we really can no longer ignore the truth that we humans are ruining our environment, and thereby ourselves.

Sowing seeds of professional doubt

The current scientific understanding of the state of our environment leaves no doubt. Yet nonetheless some do doubt the evidence. Despite the publication of a plethora of scientifically rigorous reports, the growth of many nature and environmental movements, the heightened media attention and connections with the political realm and substantial changes in thinking, there is yet to be any substantial action. Some continue to doubt the causal link between our industrialised world and lifestyle choices and the environment. Indeed, the voices of those who doubt this causal link and fear the political impact of acknowledging it has earned them the name the *merchants of doubt*.

It was the merchants of doubt and the lobbyists they nurtured, all generously paid by the scandalously profitable tobacco companies, who created confusion that obscured the facts that demonstrated the lethal properties of cigarettes. Many, many millions of deaths later, governments and consumers have begun to reverse their behaviour. Nobody believes by now that cigarettes are harmless. But still, many will not deny themselves their fag, despite the often-deadly consequences to themselves and to those around them.

Our attitude towards the importance of protecting nature has met with similar obstacles. The path has been blocked by interested parties, fossil fuel-supplying countries and related companies. Business decisions are one of the major factors that drive decisions about the environment. But many companies have great difficulty in adjusting their behaviour, even in the face of irrefutable insights. Expensive advertising campaigns by high profile petroleum brands reinforce doubts about a link between their activities and the health of the environment. Companies are driven by growth and profit, and it is in their interest to sustain growth and profit for as long as possible, even though they recognise the destructive impact of their activities on natural ecosystems, biodiversity and climate change. Big organisations release vast sums of money to mould public opinion through traditional and social media and to requisition favourable reports from pseudo-scientific think tanks. These companies bribe and otherwise hinder our political leaders and decision-makers' understanding of the facts and deprive them of the power to embark on a sustainable course.

In addition, this alliance of politicians and economic stakeholders excels at making us consumers feel that we are partly to blame. After all, it is us, the public, who want to keep driving our petrol-guzzling cars and eating our hamburgers. Following this line of reasoning, business simply follows demand and cannot do otherwise. They also appear to be masters at dismissing people who acknowledge the truth as pushy, activist lefties and twisting discussions about the value of nature into arguments about political-ideological issues. The environmental issues are being made into political fodder when the issues have little to do with politics. The issue of the environment is far more basic and profound – it is about our common interest in survival. The issue is about protecting us from our unchecked march towards unpleasant and eventually unbearable living conditions. The less fortunate amongst us will be the first to suffer the consequences.

The good news is that insightful investigative journalists, fuelled by numerous objective scientific studies and evidence, are finally managing to expose planet-destroying and deadly methodologies used by some organisations, making it increasingly clear what the problems are, who is causing them and who is responsible for perpetuating them. Science and honest journalism tell us quite clearly that the clock is ticking relentlessly, that our time is running out. If, in the next decade, we fail to phase out the habit of *growthism* in business and governments, if we fail to halve greenhouse gases and if we fail to restore natural ecosystems, our comfort zone will be severely curtailed, and we will face much misery and pain that could have been avoided.

History teaches us that things only change when not changing becomes impossible, when change becomes inevitable and unavoidable and the pressure to do nothing becomes too great. Like an inveterate smoker who finally quits after their habit leads them to an ominous visit with a cardiologist or oncologist or a COVID patient who ends up in the ICU gasping for breath and asking for a shot. Well then. Things must change! But how? How do we make sure that the knowledge that has been around for decades is transformed into inevitable and unavoidable changes that we must make, one way or the other? Let us start by listing the facts.

Blundering with nature

What facts are we dealing with that can no longer be questioned by any scientist or journalist? What has been the evolution since the

1972 publication, *Limits to Growth*? What conclusions can we draw 50 years later? Has growth slowed, stagnated or just increased? And what are the consequences? I have a feeling you already know part of the answer. But we need to see the facts in black and white. We need to confront ourselves with the magnitude of the problem. Not to make ourselves depressed or give up hope, but simply because we can only solve a problem if we understand very clearly what variables we are playing with. Fasten your seatbelts, here we go.

There are (too) many of us

There are more and more of us, and we have an increasingly destructive impact. In 1800 there were one billion of our species on this planet. It took another 124 years to reach two billion, but only 33 years to reach three billion. That is 91 years faster! And barely 15 years later, there were already four billion of us, meaning one billion people were added to the planet every 12 years. By 2021 there were more than 7.8 billion of us. According to the UN we reached 8 billion on November 15 2023 A staggering number. Too many? Another factoid. Do you have any idea how many babies are currently being born every day? Do not be shocked; there are some 380,000. An average of 160,000 people die every day. This equates to a net population growth of 220,000 people every day.

There is a bit of good news: we have reached our human growth peak. The annual population growth rate 50 years ago was 2.2% and the rate at the time of this writing stands at 1.05%. This means that it will now take a little over 12 years before the population increases by another one billion. But our delayed population growth is still an incredibly fast rate of growth. The projections, shown in billions of people on the planet by year are: eight by 2023, nine by 2038, ten by 2056 and 11 billion people by 2088.

Of course, these kinds of projections do not consider contingencies such as another world war, diseases like AIDS, a pandemic or devastating hurricanes. But sophisticated mathematics that factor in such risks are not needed to realise that even the loss of a few tens of millions of people due to manmade or natural disasters will hardly dent the projections. The numbers are profoundly sobering. How can we provide the necessities of life to such huge masses of our species without depriving other forms of life in the process?

We build and eat away

It all becomes even more hallucinatory when we consider the evolution of the world's built-up area over the last 50 years. It has increased by 22 million hectares. In the same period, 30 million hectares were added for livestock, and 160 million hectares were added for growing and unevenly distributing our food.

Nature has had to bear the brunt of this land grab without fail. Consequently, the natural ecosystems that keep our climate stable, give us healthy air and potable water, and keep most dangerous viruses within their ecological limits are being destroyed. Yet we behave as though we are oblivious to all of this. We do not heed the deafening alarms that are set off by the final death throes of so many life forms on earth. Nature may be collapsing around us. But there is no stock market listing or valuation of a share of nature.

In 1937, more than half of our planet (66%) was still wilderness, still self-governing natural ecosystems without human disturbance. By 1960, wilderness had shrunk to 62%. The decline was very fast after that: 55% in 1978, 46% in 1997 and by 2020 only 35% of the planet was estimated to be wilderness – and yes, that number includes Antarctica and the world's oceans. Thinking of all those species that are irrevocably falling out of our living engine, never to return, makes one wonder not if but when our planet will stop functioning.

Therefore, the dwindling area for wilderness cannot go without consequences. No matter how excited we are about the return of the osprey, the crane, the wolf or the otter, the state of nature is in dire straits. The recent IPBES (Intergovernmental Science-Policy Platform on Biodiversity and Ecosystem Services) report is clear. More than one million life forms are on the verge of extinction this century. This analysis is confirmed in the United Nations' fifth *Global Biodiversity Outlook 5 (GBO-5)* report (2020): none of the 20 globally agreed targets have been met.

The more wilderness we destroy and the deeper we penetrate into it, the more unpleasant the consequences we face will become. Through our western lifestyle, we are plundering our own planet, changing the biological rules of the game to the point where pathogens can no longer be contained within their own natural ecosystems.

The World Wildlife Fund's (WWF) recent report, COVID 19: Urgent Call to Protect People and Nature (2020), outlines the alarming increase in the number and frequency of new outbreaks of zoonoses, infectious diseases of vertebrates that spill over to humans. Examples include COVID, Ebola and HIV. The increase in the number of zoonotic disease outbreaks, especially since the 1960s, is a symptom of the fractured relationship between humans and nature, and the frequency of such outbreaks is rapidly increasing.

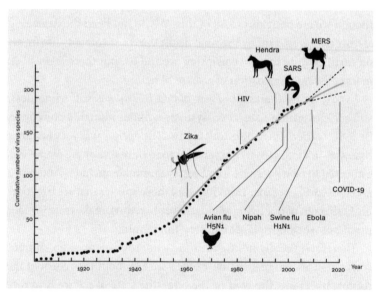

FIGURE: Evolution of human infectious virus species (1900-2020)

SOURCE: WWF / COVID 19: Urgent call to protect people and nature

Biodiversity is still in serious decline in Europe, according to the recent State of Nature in the EU (2020) report by the European Environment Agency (EEA). A quarter of Europe's wildlife is threatened with extinction, 80% of habitats are in moderate to poor condition and one third of animal and plant species are in decline. Conservation has improved for only six percent of species; for 60% it is moderate to unfavourable. Our water is in particularly bad condition; half of fish species and amphibians are declining. The 27 countries of the EU and the UK are failing to halt this decline.

The situation is bleak in the Netherlands and Flanders. The number of animals in the Netherlands' vulnerable nature reserves has fallen by half since 1990 according to the WWF's *The Living Planet Report* (2020), and the same is roughly true in agricultural areas. In Flanders, 30 per cent of plant and animal species are vulnerable or have hit the red list (*IUCN List of Endangered Species*). Even the 26% of Flemish areas that has some type of legal protection is, nonetheless, at risk: only seven percent is well managed and nature in these areas is hugely fragmented.

We massively overlook climate change

Back to being bombarded with numbers. We have not yet talked about that merciless assassin that is silently, colourlessly and for the most part odourlessly coming our way at an unprecedented speed and with an impact far greater than a hundred coronaviruses combined: climate change. Unlike the coronavirus pandemic, climate change is a relatively slow process. We like to think that the consequences will be fewer than expected. Nothing could be further from the truth. By the way, did you know that due to rapid global warming, other viruses such as the zika virus, the West Nile virus and the dengue virus are also on a rapid march towards European shores? Without decisive and quick action in the next decade, climate change will dwarf the risks of the coronavirus crisis and the social and economic disruption will be many times greater.

The negative consequences of global warming are happening before our very eyes. Extreme weather events such as hurricanes, floods and extreme drought have increased by 44% between 1980 and 2018, a near doubling with major direct and indirect consequences! Droughts are accompanied by persistent scorching heat that can lead to repeated crop failure even if water is available locally, leaving local people exhausted and malnourished. Without prospects to feed themselves, these people take refuge in nearby cities only to find that there is no work and no lodging for them, resulting in conflicts and (civil) wars. Totally disillusioned, hundreds of thousands of people once again must leave everything behind in their search for survival, their path marked with horror and pain, again resulting in conflicts and heart-breaking scenes.

According to a recent study published in the *Journal of Global Health*, by June 2022, the number of displaced people worldwide due to climate change reached a record high of more than 100 million. The Institute for Economics & Peace (IEP) predicts that around 1.2 billion people could be displaced by 2050 due to natural disasters and climate change: that is 1.2 billion times more misery and disappoint-ment. It could be worse. A new study *Quantifying the human cost of global warming* published in *Nature Sustainability* predicts that we are heading for a 2.7°C warming, with one in three people worldwide facing life in an unliveable place by the end of this century.

We are emitting too much

The consequences of an overpopulated world do not end there. Besides taking up space to live, work and meet our food needs, each person on this planet now emits on average 21% more greenhouse gases than 50 years ago, and together we emit 47% more. This is fright-ening, but a simple observation tells us that 50 years ago, there were half as many people on this planet. Is it that simple? This seems at first to be logical. Twice as many people equals twice as many emissions. It is not that simple, because only 10% of people are responsible for 50% of emissions. These numbers become hallucinatory when you consider that we all now consume 65% more meat, produce 447% more plastic and travel by air 561% more than we did 50 years ago!

When you see all these facts and figures, it is easy to become consumed by fear. We have entered an era where our human activity has taken over from natural phenomena. Earth has become primarily a planet for humans. With unprecedented speed, we are destroying precisely what keeps us alive. We determine how rivers flow, where agricultural crops grow, where pristine nature is allowed to remain. We empty the oceans of their living ecosystems and turn them into a soup of plastic. We thoughtlessly and irresponsibly consume our rare earth materials and we poison entire ecosystems with pesticides and herbicides. Under the guise of progress, we have developed forever chemicals (think of PFOS and PFAS chemicals, among others), some of which will never disappear. On top of that, our relentless addiction to fossil fuels is causing unprecedented climate disruption and the collapse of our natural ecosystems.

The rate of change in emission release is nothing short of an impressive feat, if we consider how comparatively young the human species is. On the geological time scale, the period of human civilisation represents nothing; it is but a flash in the pan. The earth is 4.6 billion years old; geological ages span millions of years but homo sapiens only appeared 250,000 years ago. As much as we applaud ourselves for our inventiveness or despise ourselves for the damage we have done, for a long time we thought we played a minor role in the big picture. Nothing could be further from the truth; our impact is ubiquitous and far-reaching. Human beings leave their fingerprints everywhere with unforeseen and often unwanted consequences. We have irrevocably entered the *age of man*, the Anthropocene. Since we humans began an advance as *masters of the universe*, we have profoundly changed the face of the planet. These have been changes for the better for many people, but we are beginning to realise that for many others these have been changes for the worse. If we can industrialise and adapt humans to embrace digital connectivity so quickly, can we turn the tide in favour of nature and ourselves?

We are tearing down biodiversity

Above all, we must realise that biodiversity loss is not just about little birds, flowers and bees. All food production thrives by the grace of biodiversity. Anyone who thinks that potatoes, cereals or tomatoes just grow everywhere with equal yields is misinformed. A lot of soils – think of deserts, for instance – are worthless for growing food. Good farmland land requires soils that are full of earthworms, insects, fungi and bacteria. Healthy soils contain more organisms than you might think. In terms of biomass, which is the total quantity or weight of organisms in a given area or volume, it averages about four to six tonnes per hectare. The bad news is that soil biodiversity is declining at a rapid pace, threatening the stability of our food production.

By the way, we too are full of various life forms. Each healthy human individual contains a hundred thousand billion microbes (microbiotics), amounting to some 1.5 kilograms per adult person. The microbiotics form cooperating ecosystems that keep us healthy both physically and mentally. More than that, we depend on them. Yep, you guessed it: our human biodiversity is also going downhill fast. So don't be mistaken when you hear reports of biodiversity decline, because it's as much about our food as it is about you and me.

We live by the delusion of the day

It is a curious phenomenon: most people know how bad our climate situation is, how biodiversity is deteriorating and how we cannot combat this and while maintaining our lifestyle, our hunger to buy and travel, our industry and agriculture. The data is irrefutable, but we adamantly continue to delude ourselves. Scientists have examined this phenomenon. A large-scale European Union survey in 2010 probed the attitude of Europeans towards biodiversity (EUROBAROMETER No 290). When participants were asked how bad they thought biodiversity loss was, 63% thought biodiversity loss was a serious global problem, 42% thought it was also a serious problem for Europe and 37% thought it was a serious problem in their own country. However, 34% had never heard of biodiversity.

Our judgment as voters and consumers is not based solely on our rational thinking. Above all, we are guided by whatever is left in our bank account at the end of the month.

Initially, I was upbeat about these findings, thinking that people were apparently aware that biodiversity loss was a serious problem. The United Nations had just announced the start of the *Decade of Biodiversity* in 2010. But my enthusiasm was soon dashed when I got my hands on the results of the general opinion survey of European Union citizens for the same year (*EUROBAROMETER No 72*).[1] What did it reveal? In order of importance, the environment, which encompassed biodiversity at the time, ranked only third from last. Unemployment was right at the top, the economic situation was second, rising prices and inflation ranked third, crime and the health system in fourth and fifth place. Interestingly, climate did not appear on the list at all in 2010. Moving forward one decade to results of the same poll conducted in 2019 and 2020, it is striking how much polls can vary, even from year to year. Immigration ranked first in 2019, environment and climate are second and the economic situation was third. But only one year later, in 2020, environment and climate dropped to place five and the economic situation suddenly ranked first again. *EUROBAROMETER No 98*, winter 2022-2023, has shown that an overwhelming majority of EU citizens support accelerating the energy transition and investing in renewable energy. Since the start of the war in Ukraine in February 2022, Europeans have wanted to reduce the EU's dependence on Russian energy sources.

Apparently, our judgment as voters and consumers is not based solely on our rational thinking. Our opinions and preferences reflect the dominant themes in the press, but above all, we are guided by whatever is left in our bank account at the end of the month. We face a wondrous set of unequivocal facts and global circumstances: uncontrollable world population growth, we are building like crazy, we are massively overlooking climate change, we are emitting greenhouse gases like madmen, we are oblivious to the fact that industry and agriculture are wiping out biodiversity, and our focus is directed by the media. We are living by the delusion of the day.

Our situation is like what the Netflix hit *Don't Look Up* humorously tries to get between our ears. Scientists discover a comet that spells the end of humanity, but no one listens to them. Everyone continues to consume and to be lulled to sleep by traditional and social media. Until it is too late...

---

1   The European Union has been surveying its residents in a standardised manner since 1974. This includes polling on the most important issues in the EU.

It's the economy, stupid

Twenty years after the publication of the Club of Rome report, we seemed to have dispensed with insights about what we were doing to the earth along with the other leftist, hippy ideas of the 1960s and 1970s. Incessantly, we all had to step back to let the economy take the stage. One-sided economic thinking took hold especially after the economic crisis of the 1980s. Republican President Ronald Reagan won elections with his rhetoric that the market was the answer to every question and a belief in neoliberal ideas that was not refuted by later democratic presidents.

During Bill Clinton's 1992 election campaign, the then young candidate uttered his now world-famous words: 'It's the economy, stupid!' His rival, incumbent President George Bush emphasised all that he had achieved in the past four years and how he would continue those policies. But that, however, was not what American voters wanted to hear. They wanted things to get better materially, more jobs, higher salaries and more prosperity. Clinton understood that very well, focused his campaign on that and won. Clinton's election slogan was and still is used by many to indicate that the economy is all-important. What the president did not yet understand – or did he? – was that power based solely on economic growth ultimately undermines the stability of the planet and its society. If you forget the intrinsic, soft and healing values, you end up facing nasty consequences. The selfish drive for more, the ideological growth mindset of neoliberalism, still rules and is averse to the finiteness and collapse of natural ecosystems.

The addiction of Industrialised Nations to growth seems to have no regard for our planet's life barometer. In the last five decades, growth trends of socio-economic parameters contrast sharply with the spectacular fall of planetary parameters. Under the ranting declarations about globalisation by many politicians and business leaders – as drivers of expanding growth and profits – we were for too long sight-blind to the causal links that were increasingly evident.

Business as usual leads to the destruction of natural ecosystems and resources. We have already learned this from the influential 1972 Club of Rome report. The world has certainly not improved in the meantime. Since then, evidence for this position has only increased. Report after report highlights the unsustainable relationship between our mainly western lifestyle and the demise of our planet. If we zoom in on the organisation of that lifestyle and neoliberalism for a moment, it quickly becomes apparent that the hunger for only more profit is becoming fatal to the viability of our planet.

The so often praised neoliberalism that promised us global market forces that made everything cheaper, with the guarantee of the same quality of services and of care, has failed. What really happened is that natural ecosystems were consistently further destroyed, product quality deteriorated significantly, and prices rose visibly. Just the opposite, in other words. A side effect was the creation of a class of the super-rich and an alarming increase in inequality.

It's the environment, stupid

It sounds logical that most people and voters are concerned with being able to earn an income or – if we look at it globally – with simply being able to survive from day to day. In a world where nature is seen as a given, from which we get to reap for free, that is logical. But even more logically, of course, it is nonsense to think that we don't need to include nature in the cost. Of course, nature also has its value, its price.

However wedded we may be to our western lifestyle, we cannot ignore the fact that we cannot sustain it with traditional fossil fuels, with the continued growth of consumption and the ongoing destruction of our environment. Nature has never been free and is becoming less so by the day. Keep in mind that the costs of externalities are often not passed back to the responsible parties. I will explain this point by using the tobacco industry, again, as an example. Tobacco companies produce the poison, but taxpayers bear the cost of medical care for smokers. Likewise, the cost of the negative impacts of fossil fuel production and use is not passed on to oil producers. Easy as pie, they are allowed to continue polluting humans and the planet almost undisturbed. The government – i.e., we as taxpayers – end up paying for an ever-increasing and unjustifiable cost. Even today, oil companies continue to destroy thousands of hectares of natural ecosystems with impunity. But if a garage owner discharges his oil into a stream, the fine is – quite rightly – considerable. The polluter pays! A fine principle, but apparently not applicable to everyone. 'All pigs are equal, but some pigs are more equal than others': maybe we should reread George Orwell's *Animal Farm* after all?

Returning to the example of fossil fuels, the obvious question is why governments are so hesitant to phase out fossil fuels now that their impact on natural ecosystems and the climate is known. Looking through a purely economic lens makes several things clear. You may not be surprised to learn that governments are also big earners and generate a lot of revenue through our addiction to oil, just as they do through collecting excise tax on cigarettes, alcohol and petroleum products. Every time we refuel, the till rings for the government. The proceeds of excise taxes – which generate billions – are used by many governments to finance part of society. This ensures that the government's budget is sufficient to finance expenditures that can mollify voters.

Not surprisingly, a lot of politicians have a hard time deciding to move away from our fossil addiction. Lobby groups and *merchants of doubt* explain the folly of such a move to politicians. After all, how would the government make up for the lost revenue? Slowly but steadily, the tide is turning. Increasingly, politicians are realising that some traditional systems must be put aside, and that tax income can be recouped in other ways.

Just about every country is thinking about the greening of its tax system whereby disappearing or dying sources of tax are compensated for in the future. These green tax reforms will have to be accelerated in the coming years. It is now becoming increasingly clear, not only to scientists, but also to policymakers and journalists, that a society based on renewable energy can deliver more than the current tax mechanisms on fossil fuels. Although green tax reforms will benefit the planet, they alone are not enough.

Saving ourselves and the planet requires much more ambition and perseverance. It also requires courage. It is courage that has driven our accomplishment so far. Without it we would still be sitting in caves around a campfire. The stone age ended not because there were no more stones, but because new opportunities presented themselves and humanity dared to embrace them. Putting an end to the fossil fuel era does not have to wait until the last drop of oil or the last bits of coal are used up. The accords of the Paris climate agreement require that half of all currently known coal reserves must remain in the ground.

It is becoming increasingly clear, not only to scientists, but also to policymakers and journalists, that a society based on renewable energy can deliver more than the current tax mechanisms on fossil fuels.

The dream we have never dreamt before

Now, at the dawn of the Anthropocene, we have arrived at a time when we must dare to make new fundamental and radical changes to our systems. It is humanity's greatest challenge ever. The choices we will make in the next decade will determine whether we, our children, our grandchildren and all other life forms on earth have a future. Our greatest challenge is not whether we have the right knowledge or whether we can develop the technology we will need to succeed. Our biggest challenge is time. Can we make the right decisions, can we choose and take the right path in time? We cannot afford any more missteps. A decision made too late is a bad decision. A wrong decision remains wrong even if everyone clings to the known and destructive systems, just as a right decision remains right if only a few behave accordingly. But the tide is turning...

Natural disasters are climate disasters

In June 2022, northeast India and Bangladesh were ravaged by heavy rains and floods. In some places, twice the normal amount of rain fell resulting in floods and landslides. There were dozens of deaths. Four million people needed urgent help. Four million! Normal weather patterns seem disrupted as extreme heat and drought are often accompanied by massive rainfall. We saw a similar phenomenon in

May 2023 in the Emilia-Romagna region of northern Italy. A long period of drought was followed by a deluge. In a day and a half, more rain fell than what is normal over six months. Forty thousand people had to be evacuated. In my own region too, everything suddenly changed in the summer of 2021 and the true face of the dangerous consequences of climate change became grimly clear. The eastern half of Belgium, the Dutch province of Limburg and the German federal states of Rhineland-Palatinate and North Rhine-Westphalia faced a veritable *water bomb* – a locally suspended low-pressure area between two high-pressure regions – with particularly high amounts of precipitation and heavy flooding. More than 200 people were killed.

The press continues to wrongly describe these events as terrible natural disasters, but this vocabulary is factually incorrect. We are witnessing repeated manmade *climate disasters*. These events are not caused by a natural phenomenon. They result from a man-made catastrophe called climate change. It is high time to adjust our vocabulary and systematically talk about climate disasters instead of natural disasters. Natural disasters are natural phenomena, climate disasters are man-made.

'This is the last call ...' said UN Secretary-General António Guterres following the IPCC's *Sixth Assessment Report* (2023). This latest synthesis report to 2030 does not lie:

- climate risks will occur faster and will be more severe
- there is an immense difference between 1.5 and 2°C of warming
- the risk of developing mutually reinforcing and irreversible *tipping points* will rapidly increase
- once we surpass 1.5 degrees of warming the possibilities and effectiveness of climate adaptation will shrink
- the dangerous impact of climate change such as hurricanes, heat waves, floods will increase not linearly but exponentially.

Keep in mind that climate adaptation only mitigates the symptoms; it is not a structural solution. There is only one solution, and that is to get rid of our CO_2 emissions as soon as possible.

Lessons to be learned from the COVID *pandemic*

There is a big difference between stating ambitions and implementing them. This was made clear at the 2022 United Nations Climate Change Conference, COP27, in Sharm-el-Sheikh, Egypt. An agreement, not worthy of the name, was reached at the very last minute. The topic under debate was the creation of a Loss and Damage Fund to compensate vulnerable countries for the effects they encountered from climate change. But, as at previous COP meetings, no progress was made on the pivotal topics, such as exiting from all fossil fuels. A lot will have to be done in the coming years to rectify this. In any case, substantial progress does not look promising, because the next climate summit, COP 28, will be organised at the end of 2023 in Dubai, a Gulf state living on oil and gas extraction. The United Arab Emirates (UAE) has appointed Dr Sultan Ahmed Al Jaber as chairman of the upcoming climate summit, an eminent fossil energy advocate.

It appears that a balanced budget remains more important than a planet out of balance. Unfortunately, the consequences of the planet's collapse are still too indirect to take abrupt action, and the appetite for mere economic gain has not yet been satisfied. The COVID pandemic landed us in an existential crisis, with the survival of the human race suddenly elevated to a main concern. Its cause was obvious, and the consequences swift and pernicious. Because of that, and remarkably quickly, any discussion of the affordability of measures disappeared, and additional financial resources could easily be tapped by borrowing more money and keeping the cost out of the regular annual budgets. The pandemic forced rapid and far-reaching decisions to be taken and implemented, and forced behaviours to be changed. In the bat of an eye, governments around the world acted, and the results of their actions came more rapidly than expected. Which means that we should ask ourselves: which actions could induce a tipping point on behalf of the environment? Can any lessons from the coronavirus pandemic serve as game-changers? Does this coronavirus offer us a template on which to build a strategy to change behaviours and attitudes, engineer systemic change and elicit action?

Do we dare to learn lessons and see the world differently? Do we dare to look at the little bird behind the elephant? Can we, globally, begin to apply the protective power of social distancing to nature by giving her back her space, respecting her need to operate without human interference? Can we learn to distance ourselves from that which keeps us alive?

Do we put on glasses with black, grey or pink lenses?

If we look to the future through black glasses, we see the collapse of our society and planet looming in our future. After we are gone, borne away on gloomy clouds, a deluge will follow, in other words. Through grey glasses, we see many intentions and few too actions spread over too long a period. This is frightening, because in the past, big changes were often announced with great fanfare to cover up the great inaction. We have come to realise that policymakers and governments may well be confronted with challenges that impede them from implementing their own decisions. And this is where young people play a remarkably crucial role. I will limit myself to two examples, but there are so many other young heroes who 'dare' to fight the battle for sustainability. Canadian Severn Suzuki addressed world leaders at the Earth Summit in Rio de Janeiro in 1992 as a 12-year-old girl. She said: 'It is not what you say, it is what you do'! For the first time, a young person addressed world leaders with an unmistakable message. Her speech reinforced the call for more focus on sustainability and partly led to the Kyoto Protocol in 1997, the forerunner of today's climate agreement. Severn Suzuki certainly reinforced intentions, but unfortunately not yet deeds. However, another teenager managed to spark a global movement. Climate activist Greta Thunberg's speech at the 2019 World Climate Summit, four years after the Paris climate summit, went a step further. She snarled at world leaders: 'How dare you! You have stolen my dreams and my childhood with your empty words!' She confronted world leaders with their inaction. Through her simple and personal initiative in Sweden, she now symbolises a movement of millions and is given speaking time at all climate-related world forums. I hope from the bottom of my heart that her outrage and words have initiated the necessary change.

Looking through rose-coloured glasses, there is also good news to report. Within the United Nations, world leaders are becoming increasingly convinced that further destruction of our planet must stop, that only universal objectives and bold and sustained action can lead to a sustainable future. Major new global agreements, coupled with systematic monitoring and adjustment, support attempts to turn the tide. Examples include the UN *Sustainable Development Goals*, the UN *Paris Climate Agreement* and the UN *Kunming-Montreal Biodiversity Agreement*. Top figures in international finance, meanwhile, are also warning explicitly about the economic dangers of climate change. The statement in 2019 by Christine Lagarde, the then managing director of the International Monetary Fund (IMF) still reverberates: 'Unless we take action on climate change, future generations will be roasted, toasted, fried and grilled.'

The Word Economic Forum's latest *Global Risk Report* is dominated by nature and environmental issues, and there seems to be a realisation that business as usual is no longer an option for the future. The EU *Green Deal* – the EU's policy plan – is based on a socially responsible and green transition. Including climate neutrality by 2050, an expansion of protected natural areas to 30% and the establishment of a sustainable food system. And yes, the circular economy is also registered as a priority in the *European Green Deal* targets. The first signs of a *value rotation* – the moment when shareholders and investors change their perspectives and expectations in perfect synchronisation – is emerging, and there is a growing movement that chooses sustainability, solidarity and quality over self-interest and profit.

Nine planetary boundaries

The solution is often found within the error. Or in the words of *Anthem*, a beautiful song by Leonard Cohen: 'There is a crack in everything, that's how the light gets in.' The way that we organise our economy will determine the likelihood of success. The study of economics is a relatively young science and the understanding of it

We will have to go through a systemic transition, to an economy that is regenerative, in which any new product is designed to perform indefinitely. has undergone considerable changes in the last 100 years; this is expected to continue. The planet-destroying linear disposable economy gave way to the recycling economy and is moving (too slowly) towards the circular economy, where planetary limits and the finite nature of many resources are basic conditions.

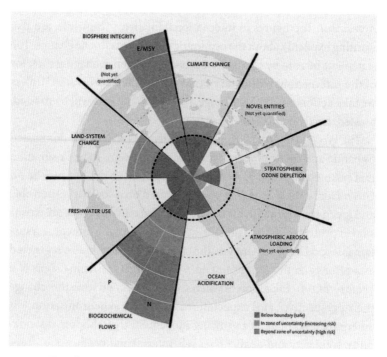

FIGURE: The nine planetary boundaries

SOURCE: J. Lokrantz/Azote, based on Steffen et al. 2015

The insight that the earth has *planetary limits* that we cannot cross with impunity is attributed to Johan Rockström, the Swedish professor who is internationally recognised as an expert on global sustainability issues. The principle is that to continue making sustainable use of our planet's resources, we as humanity must stay within the nine planetary boundaries. If we cross those boundaries, abrupt and even irreversible environmental changes may occur that could make life very difficult or even impossible for many people, plants and animals. Four of the nine planetary boundaries have already been crossed due to human activities: climate change, biodiversity loss, altered land systems (land system change) and altered biochemical cycles (phosphorus and nitrogen). Climate change and biodiversity loss constitute the Core Boundaries. By transgressing these dramatically, we put the whole of our planet in a new and potentially irreversible state.

Because we have crossed the planetary boundaries, we will have to go through a systemic transition to an economy that is regenerative. That is, an economy that gives back more than what it takes and where new products are not designed to self-destruct and planned obsolescence is unknown, when products are designed to perform indefinitely. An economy where even waste will increasingly be seen as a raw material for new products. An economy where a product's lifetime performance (its fitness) is incorporated into the design and is based on performance and sustainability throughout its life cycle.

This is a kind of reversal mechanism where we will buy fewer and fewer products and more and more services. For instance, in the future, we will no longer buy TVs but 'viewing hours'; no longer buy cars but 'mobility'; no light bulbs but *lighting hours*. Successful TV, car and light manufacturers will henceforth offer high-quality, sustainable and regenerative TVs and cars. We will no longer pay for a product, but for a performance. Say you buy 450,000 kilometres of mobility or 100,000 hours of light. In both cases, the manufacturer will design and provide you with a car or light bulb that can perform for as long as possible in terms of performance and quality. Rather the same car that runs for 450,000 kilometres than three cars that run for 150,000 kilometres and rather one lamp that burns for 100,000 hours than 200 lamps that only burn for 2,500 hours each.

There is still some way to go, but the first, highly successful models with system-changing features already exist. More and more companies are following *cradle to cradle* principles where waste is seen as a raw material for new products. The world's largest taxi company no longer has cars (Uber), the world's largest hotel company no longer has hotels (Airbnb), the world's largest internet provider no longer has computers (Google), and the world's largest film and TV series provider does not make its own programmes and certainly does not sell TVs (Netflix). Time is running out, but the next few years will be unusually exciting.

The success and system-changing power of this reversal mechanism will depend on the extent to which civic initiatives (bottom-up) and international public policy (top-down) can reinforce and accelerate each other, where government legislative initiatives can be quickly activated, where entrepreneurs as well as investors actively participate, and where a large community support base is created.

The choice is ours. When nothing is certain, anything is possible. With the knowledge present in nature, gained from over 4.5 billion years of existence, with all its research, development and trial-and-error, there is so much to learn from our planet Earth, our hotel with not four- or five-star, but million-star reviews. No, the choice is not about a return to the past. We can choose to move forward to a sustainable future. A future where innovation and smart technology go hand in hand with the restoration and preservation of natural ecosystems. Where the circular and regenerative economy protects the planet and renewable energy is connected globally. Where our food supply is sustainable, and our society is open, warm and inclusive. Where our dependence on nature is self-evident and recognised as a human right.

It should be clear by now that our near future is not about moving a few pawns, it involves taking bold historic and strategic steps. To survive, we need the actions of great leaders like we have seen more than once in the past.

From Moonshot to Earthshot

A giant leap towards a healthy world

In 1961, the newly elected US President John F. Kennedy challenged his nation to put a man on the moon in the next decade. He did so because the Soviet Union, America's Cold War rival, had made spectacular achievements in space exploration and under no circumstances did Kennedy want the Soviet Union to be the first to land a man or woman on the moon. Kennedy was convinced that with a strong commitment from the American people and industry, America would win the space race. Speaking at Rice University in the Texan city of Houston a year later, on 12 September 1962, he explained why: 'We choose to go to the moon. We choose to go to the moon in this decade and do the other things, not because they are easy, but because they are hard, because that goal will serve to organise and measure the best of our energies and skills, because that challenge is one that we are willing to accept, one that we are unwilling to postpone, and one which we intend to win ...'

What a wonderful statement: 'We choose to go to the moon.' This is not just an ambition, or a wish. It is a clearly stated choice to take action. In the ensuing years, an estimated 400,000 people and 20,000 companies would collaborate on the project, which at current value would have cost some USD 135 billion. In less than a decade, on 20 July 1969 at 22:56 to be precise, astronaut Neil Armstrong became the first human to set foot on the moon. As he placed his left foot on the surface of the moon, he uttered the now world-famous words: 'That's one small step for man, one giant leap for mankind.' Kennedy's speech at Rice University in 1962 is also known as the Moonshot speech. Its power and strength lies mainly in the fact that the president dared to make a clear choice. A difficult choice that would lead to success through the commitment of his nation. With his Moonshot, Kennedy proved two things: it is possible to change, and it is possible to achieve results quickly – within a decade. Change begins by approaching reality in a new way and seeing possibilities rather than limitations.

We are currently at a point in history where we are beginning to approach reality in a new way, as we have done many times before in history. In the times of the Greeks and Romans, in the Middle Ages and the Renaissance, during the time of the great scientific discoveries in the seventeenth and eighteenth centuries, again during the Industrial Revolution in the nineteenth century, and finally in the twentieth century, a time of new ideas about the place of humans in the universe. Who are we really in relation to nature and how do we literally and figuratively appreciate and nourish that natural environment? How do we calculate the value of nature and include it in our forecasts? How do we demonstrate the added value of investing in this asset? How do we show that without investing in nature, all other assets lose all of their value?

We are now on the verge, forced by reality, of looking at the world in a different way, this time nature inclusive. Many still feel lord and master of the planet, but more and more people are coming to the realisation that we need to change the way we live. We must live in cooperation with nature and in cooperation with each other to survive, together. How weird the world looks now, and strange this phase of history will appear when we look back a few decades from now. Let me explain what I mean by reviewing how the pharmaceutical industry works at present: Naturally derived products have historically played a major role in the development of pharmaceuticals, in a manner akin to a collaboration with the ingenuity of nature. The pharmaceutical industry has extracted knowledge and chemical structures from nature from which it has made billions, but nature has not received anything in return. What is their contribution to the resource, what do they give back to nature? Logically, it should be the responsibility of the pharmaceutical producers to pay a contribution for the profits that nature provided them for free. That seems obvious.

To find out how big that contribution could be, I looked up the average cost for taking a drug from the stage of discovery through research and development, ready to be launched worldwide – between USD 2-3 billion on average – and met with a prominent figure in the pharmaceutical industry, Belgian Paul Stoffels, Vice-Chairman of the Executive Committee and Chief Scientific Officer at Johnson & Johnson's Janssen Pharmaceutical Companies. When I asked him if he agreed that many medicines still have their origins in nature, he immediately confirmed this. He could also agree with my next question about the average investment for drug development. But my next question was met with a friendly laugh: 'If you believe that nature is important for health, are you willing to give half of the investment cost of one medicine to the nature sector?' As important as he thought this issue was, a financial collaboration is not possible in the current economic context nor within current share holder structures. 'But if you can convince the shareholders, there's a chance,' he added. You may now think this is a bland answer, but it was anything but bland. It forced me to rethink how the world works. Even when it comes to health, the laws of economic growth and profit maximisation are predominant.

My conversation with Paul also taught me another, perhaps even more important lesson: the pharmaceutical world mainly makes money from sick people and bigger numbers of sick people equals bigger revenues. You do not have to be a prodigy to realise that there are also many sectors that make money mainly from healthy people. Much of the insurance sector is completely focused on healthy people. The sector is structured as a kind of solidarity system, with many people paying an annual premium to insure themselves against damages. Damages such as car accidents, theft, fire, water damage and so on, as well as interventions for illness and so-called life insurance. The less the insurance companies ultimately must pay out in case of accidents or catastrophes, the more of their revenue they retain. Also, the longer people stay healthy, the more revenue. In short: the pharmaceutical industry earns from sick people, the insurance industry from healthy people. This seems like an opportunity to be explored, the logical question being: could the insurance sector contribute to keeping people and nature healthy?

With this concept in mind, I arrived full of confidence for a pitch to Allianz Germany, the largest insurer in the world. They are so powerful and rich that even Bayern Munich's football stadium, Allianz Arena, is named after the company. In spring 2023 Allianz

> The pharmaceutical world mainly makes money from the sick. The more (treatable) sick there are, the bigger the revenues.

paid EUR 130 million to extend their contract for this right until 2033. My proposal to Allianz was this: 'You have a football stadium, why don't you have a national park? If you are serious about insuring lives, surely you would be better off investing in restoring nature and climate?' The Allianz representatives straightened up in their chairs and remarked that they found my question extremely relevant. After all, how ethical is an insurer if they do not invest in things that ensure life? I heard nothing more from Allianz after that meeting, although an insider told me recently that the company was taking the first steps towards financing a large-scale bee conservation project.

Incidentally, I also discovered in the interim that insurance companies invest their assets. Their investments are not in the form of, for example, the restoration and protection of nature or the climate but rather in things like underground car parks, 'because they return the most value', according to a top executive at a Belgian insurance company. Rather balance the numbers than balance a planet. This mindset has characterised and dominated our western society for far too long. A song by Joni Mitchell echoes in my head: 'They paved paradise and put up a parking lot.'

'You only start seeing it when you realise it' was a typical expression of Dutch footballer Johan Cruijff. Also, once you see it, you can hardly imagine seeing it any other way. If you know the benefits nature provides for our health, it is surely incomprehensible that we continue to destroy nature. Restoring our relationship with nature should be a priority. Not just in words, but especially in deeds. The relationship between health and nature is and will remain inextricably linked. And perhaps we should approach this connection differently and turn it into a new health model that increases the quality of life and creates many new jobs. As we discover that health is much more than not being sick and establish that nature is the most powerful medicine, we urgently need to create connections and build collaborations between nature and the healthcare sector. Proposals for effective mechanisms to make that happen are welcome and I am eager to activate the process. Who wants to join me?

Nature as the main healer

Since the beginning of time nature and science have formed an inseparable unity. This union is reflected in the contemporary practice of the pharmaceutical industry. I have personal experience of this. In November 2014, I was at the World Parks Congress of the International Union for the Conservation of Nature (IUCN) at Sidney Olympic Park in Australia. More than 5,000 nature experts participated in this important world congress that takes place once every 10 years. The central theme of the congress was *Parks, People, Planet: inspiring solutions*. As president of EUROPARC Federation, I had been asked to lead one of the eight sub-themes, *Improving health and wellbeing*. My task – spread over several days – was to lead the talks and discussions on the relationship between nature, health and wellbeing and convey the conclusions to the plenary.

Increasingly, nature organisations were demonstrating the positive results of the relationship between nature and health. The media had become interested in the subject. Media reports about it were on the increase, to the degree that the topic had taken on the characteristics of a global conquest. In parallel, new and very convincing scientific evidence was being released, so one of the aims of the conference was to link the two sectors more closely. During a preliminary discussion, Dr William Jackson, director of Parks Victoria, asked me to pull out all the stops to get the connection of nature and health into the final conclusions of the conference. Parks Victoria had been experimenting with a new programme 'Healthy Parks, Healthy People' (HPHP) in Australia for a while, and it was an instant success. I sensed that nature and health could be a formula for success. My convictions suddenly got a huge boost of confidence when Dr Jonathan Patz, Director of the Global Health Institute at the University of Wisconsin-Madison, walked to the lectern and began his keynote presentation. From the first word his presentation was spot on. A world authority in his field, Patz opened with the following statement: 'Protected areas can save more lives than the public health sector can achieve.' He hit the proverbial nail straight on its head. Remember, this was not a statement by a conservationist or the theory of a professor. These were the words of an authority from the medical world. Nature – biodiversity – can save more lives than the health sector. It sounds simple and, in fact, it is.

For tens of thousands of years, we have consulted nature to develop medicines, as disease prevention and to promote our wellbeing. Although modern pharmaceutical science has strayed far from its ancient roots, biodiversity remains an essential source and vital supplier of medicines. For healing and health restoration, we remain very dependent on nature. About 70% of drugs developed and marketed in the US in the last 25 years were derived from natural products. This makes nature a free supplier of our health!

To date, plants have been the source of most medicinal products derived from nature. We are still discovering new possibilities every day in species and organisms that are biologically and chemically incredibly diverse, as for example in snakes, frogs, a whole number of arthropods and fungi. The preservation of biodiversity is therefore vital for the successful discovery and development of drugs in the future. In the case of drug discovery, according to some estimates, loss of biodiversity leads to the loss of at least one important drug every two years. But with the rate of extinction of so many species – more than 1 million species are threatened with extinction this century – we are also losing the traditional knowledge of medicinal uses which, in the long run, also endangers human survival. Species gone; knowledge gone. With every piece of habitat that disappears under the plough or concrete, we impoverish nature and rob ourselves of potential medicines.

There are lots of examples of medicines that are a direct result of nature's ingenuity. One such example is Mexico's national icon and perhaps the most famous salamander in the world, the axolotl. It is a little animal that seems to be able to work magic. This eccentric creature lives mainly underwater and remains in larval stage throughout its life. It is a somewhat creepy-looking, mostly white salamander with a friendly looking face and pink external, stem-like gills. Axolotls are invaluable to medicine. In the early 20th century, they were crucial in understanding how organs develop and function in vertebrates. They helped scientists identify the causes of 'spina bifida' in humans, a birth defect in which the spine does not form properly. And they played a role in the discovery of thyroid hormones. But the axolotl's most fascinating contribution to science is in the field of regenerative medicine. The animals can grow missing limbs, tails, organs, parts of the eye and even parts of the brain. This is the magic that is apparently common in nature. Biologists have been trying to identify the mechanisms behind the axolotls' regenerative abilities for decades. Many scientists hypothesise that this is because they carry a trait from their embryonic stages into their larval existence. Their regenerative ability appears to diminish with age, although other salamanders seem to be able to regenerate even as adults. Thanks to its unique physiology and remarkable ability to regenerate severed limbs, the axolotl has become an important laboratory model for everything from tissue repair to treating errors in development and cancer.

The axolotl is just one of many, many examples of animals or plants that have helped us medicinally. With the extinction of species, opportunities for medicine and the development of new drugs are shrinking. The next time you end up in hospital or visit the doctor or pharmacist, consider for a moment that behind all those treatments, prescriptions and medicine boxes there is a world of biodiversity. You need to realise that the impact of the current global decline in biodiversity will eventually become visible and palpable in the treatment of diseases, and in the availability and curative power of our future medicines. In just over a century, we have almost completely lost our deep relationship with nature; we have forgotten that we are a part of that same nature. A lesson in humility would not go amiss as we experience first-hand the consequences of our overbearing and destructive attitude towards nature.

Meanwhile, we are eroding biodiversity bit by bit, and with it we are destroying the potential for letting nature help us to keep ourselves healthy. No less than 13.7 million people worldwide died in 2016 because of living or working in an unhealthy environment, accounting for 24% of all deaths, according to the latest published figures from the World Health Organisation (WHO) – note that this report predates the

COVID pandemic which killed almost seven million people worldwide as of spring 2023. Another WHO report concluded that nine in 10 people live in regions with polluted air. It is believed that over four million people die annually from breathing polluted outdoor air.

At the other end of the spectrum, scientific evidence about the positive effects of the human relationship with nature continues to accumulate. When we restore our relationship with nature, not only do we become healthier physically, but nature also provides excellent medicine mentally. Many scientific studies show that physical contact with nature reduces the incidence of heart attacks and strokes by 20 to 30%, diabetes by up to 40% and depression by up to 30%. The use of nature to treat depression and burnout has been gaining tremendous importance in recent years. A Harvard Medical School study reported the particularly positive effects of a walk in the woods for 20 to 30 minutes, three times each week. Nature makes us healthy, without demanding anything in return other than being allowed to exist. Evidence is accumulating that psychological stress is reduced by visiting green spaces and being exposed to a natural environment. Joe Dispenza, the world-renowned chiropractor, states that it has been proven in clinical studies that two hours of natural sounds a day reduces stress hormones by up to 800 per cent and activates 500-600 DNA segments known to be responsible for healing and repairing the body.

With all the new science-based insights and evidence, we are becoming more and more convinced that nature in its many guises is a powerful and almost-free regenerative medicine. A forest remains a forest, can sustain itself naturally and can offer us clean air 24/7. It costs next to nothing and offers great benefits. More and more doctors are becoming convinced and are willing to prescribe a dose of nature. A cheaper prescription for health is difficult to imagine. It is a direct result of *Healthy Parks, Healthy People*, which I became convinced of in Australia and which I am now trying to roll out in Europe with EUROPARC Federation: increasingly, doctors regard a dose of nature as a preventative and sometimes curative wonder drug for some ailments.

Nature as therapy could get much more interesting. For instance, I have been looking for a physiotherapist or *kinesiotherapist of nature* for some time. I use the phrase metaphorically to make my thesis clear. What happens if, for example, you seriously sprain your foot while playing sports? You go to the doctor or emergency room, an MRI or CT scan is taken, your foot might be immobilised in a cast but eventually you end up at the physiotherapist.

We must realise that the current decline in biodiversity will eventually be felt in our ability to treat disease, and in the availability and curative power of our future medicines.

And after 10, 20 or 30 treatments, you are declared cured. Meanwhile, the well-oiled system of exquisite care and treatment by medically well-trained people and the administrative and financial dealings are all neatly arranged. As an alternative, you might be prescribed a medical cure in nature. Perhaps a national park ranger or a nature guide would monitor your progress. Would a cost-benefit analysis of the nature therapeutic compared to the conventional approach help to value nature, and therefore to protect nature?

By thinking only in terms of medicines and clinical treatments, we sideline the best doctor, which is nature. Nature is barely mentioned in medical training – a missed opportunity. By making a medical nature component mandatory in both university and college courses, science and patients benefit. There would be enormous merit in establishing a professional framework to record and share knowledge arising from the rapidly growing number of medics who prescribe 'nature by prescription' preventively and curatively. Training of medics and paramedics who can make expert judgements on both health promotion and improvement of the disease process is needed. Nature as medicine represents a tremendous opportunity in terms of health and value when nature as medicine is finally appreciated. For every treatment with or in nature, fair compensation is due to nature: the patient benefits, the treating doctor benefits and nature benefits. A win-win-win result in quality of life, in economic stability and sustainability.

Leadership in times of crisis

In preparation for the Paris World's Fair (1889) and a hundred years after the storming of the Bastille that initiated the French Revolution,

Gustave Eiffel went to the mayor of Paris to persuade him to build an iron tower. The design included a steep rise to a slender pinnacle that the engineers were confident they could safely achieve, but the project could have easily been seen as an iron castle in the air. Just imagine if the mayor of Paris had said: 'A 324-metre-high iron tower? There is no support for that.' What would Paris be without the Eiffel Tower; Egypt without the pyramids of Giza; India without the Taj Mahal? These may be somewhat contradictory and tendentious statements, but the decisions to erect these monuments were based on conviction, love and support. Love and conviction can engender support from others for issues, decision, or projects. Waiting for support can sometimes be convenient as an excuse for inaction. But in the current context, invoking a lack of sufficient support is no longer an option. It sometimes comes down to showing leadership and just going for it.

I began this section with Kennedy's famous speech and his belief that a trip to the moon was feasible within a decade. This Moonshot, the decision to go to the moon, mobilised everyone. A huge amount of money was released and with it, much brainpower and enthusiasm from many people. And together, they succeeded. We are in a similar situation today. Our planet is literally and figuratively on fire and there is a need for rapid intervention that allows for sustainable system change.

We know what the causes are and what the consequences of inaction will be, and we have good clues on how to turn this precarious situation around.

The danger lies not in knowledge gaps nor funding shortfalls. The danger lies in the depth of our universal will, courage and the short time we have left to get the job done.

President Kennedy showed with Moonshot that if a nation firmly wanted to be first on the moon, it was possible to achieve it within 10 years. It is time to opt for an Earthshot, a new universal plan in which everyone – from world leaders and spiritual leaders to captains of industry to citizens – has only one goal in mind:
We have 10 years to save the planet.

This means:

- reducing greenhouse gases by at least half by 2030
- halting the loss of biodiversity
- reserving 30 to 50% of the planet as protected natural areas

This is not just a moral effort. Our very existence on this planet is at stake. Failure equals misery, disaster and the demise of the human presence on this planet. There is a need for a recruiting narrative in which it becomes clear to everyone that without swift common action, we are well on our way to destroying precisely what keeps us alive. Our planet does not need humans to survive, but we humans cannot survive without a liveable planet. Starting in earnest and in time, and that means now, can ensure that costs are contained. Waiting only increases the degree of technical challenge, increases the costs dramatically and increases the likelihood of failure.

Despite great advances in knowledge, biodiversity and climate change are often in the losing camp. We are getting better at fighting the consequences, but we prevaricate and hesitate to resolutely launch the necessary systemic and sustainable transitions to address the causes. The success of an Earthshot will largely depend on the extent to which governments dare to make a choice, design tools and legislate.

Every individual effort is important and desirable, but making real strides can only be done through government leadership. Why are governments so important? The main reason is that governments set the rules of the game. Because the scope of government policies can cover whole territories, every national is part of it and governments can organise enforcement policies – control of implementation. Taxes apply to everyone, and no one should drive through red lights. Imagine if such obligations and rules were to be obeyed only on a voluntary basis. I doubt that many would pay their full tax bill or any tax at all and I wonder how many road casualties there would be.

Placing all responsibility and trust in politicians and governments alone to save our planet is no guarantee of success. And Donald Trump is by no means the only climate denier or nature destroyer. Everyone will have to be convinced of the added value. The extent to which all stakeholders can be acknowledged and recognised is therefore an

Our planet does not need humans to survive, but we humans cannot do without a liveable planet. essential and a powerful tool to get everyone on board and will require tailor-made education, policies and agreements relevant to their particular location. After all, our relationship to nature is not the same everywhere, if only because of different cultural and religious backgrounds. Whereas a lot of cultures and religions advocate a deeper and more respectful connection with nature, our predominant Christian and western society is characterised by a clearly anthropocentric, selfish attitude. We are above nature, as it were. Nature is our property, a consumer good, that is how it is seen. There are certainly signs that the tide is turning: the dominant traditional idea that we are the centre of the universe is crumbling. We are not the centre of the universe, but together we can secure our own habitat, if we show the leadership needed to do so. The idea that we are not above nature but part of it is gaining ground and slowly we are moving from ego to eco.

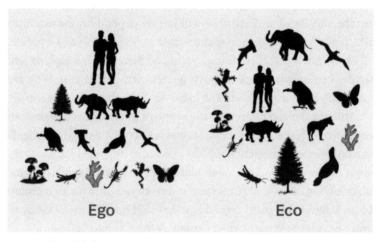

Ego   Eco

FIGURE: *The shift from ego to eco*

But how do you get an Earthshot done if everyone must participate; everyone from all cultures, all countries and all religions? How will we get everyone on board if we do not decide on it together and there is also no sanction if we don't comply? I personally think that the complexity and diversity of today's global community are both a handicap and an asset in this transition. President Kennedy was able to get the whole American nation on board with his targeted policy choice, demonstrating how important leadership within governments can be in a systemic transition. But can you think of another Moonshot? Have any more of these system transitions ever taken place? I routinely run a small quiz when speaking to audiences of decision makers. The audience can include government leaders to town counsellors. I ask them if they know of or have been part of systemic changes in which governments played a significant role. Sometimes they remain deafeningly silent. Yet I have learned of several systemic changes that have occurred in the past.

Businesses can be surprisingly agile in response to government initiatives. For instance, Belgian Étienne Lenoir built the first car with a combustion engine powered by coal gas, in 1862. Only few years later, the first cars with internal combustion engines that ran on petrol were produced. After that, innovations came thick and fast. The first mass-produced petrol fuelled car, the Model T, rolled off Ford's production line in 1908. Only five years later, Ford Motor Company sold 189,088 units of its Model T automobile. Photos of New York in 1900 show thoroughfares dominated by horse drawn carts and carriages, and only a few cars. By 1913 the situation had been totally reversed and the horse and cart were the exceptions. The advent of cars solved the logistic problem of removing huge mountains of horse manure from the streets of New York, London, Paris and elsewhere. Cars were considered a cleaner form of transportation than horses, all made possible by a government that invested in logistics and in the future.

The number of car manufacturers proliferated during the last century and now there are about 1,000 different car brands and an estimated 1.4 billion cars on the planet. It was not just the performance and design of Ford or Mercedes or Volkswagen vehicles that stimulated this proliferation: it was the construction of roads, fully funded by governments (taxpayers). Politicians and governments adopted policies and agreed budgets for road construction. The roads provided freedom of access and their construction provided employment and reduced welfare burdens. The choice to build transportation infrastructures was an unprecedented example of systemic transformation and job creation, unaware as we were of the disastrous consequences of emissions from the exponentially growing car fleet.

Consider the other infrastructures we have created; systemic infrastructure interventions enabled by governments, such as aviation and maritime aviation or maritime infrastructures. Governments have invested massively in air and seaports and in infrastructures to support oil and gas, electricity, and water supply. In each case governments have been responsible for building and financing infrastructures that benefited us as consumers but also industry as suppliers. Little or no consideration was given to the ecological problems caused by these investments. This was a design mistake we must never repeat.

These infrastructure projects have shown that when governments and the populace dare to make choices, massive projects can be undertaken and completed successfully. What stops governments from fully investing today in renewable energy networks, restoring natural ecosystems and legislating measures to stimulate the development of a circular economy? Is it fear of job losses or decreases in tax revenues? Gone are the days when a politician dared not opt for sustainability because he knew he would be electorally punished for it. Hesitation and the short-term thinking of many politicians are unfounded and there is no longer any argument to defend inaction.

Governments are often unaware or insufficiently informed about the innovative and guiding role they can play. Politicians, non-elected officials and industry partners conclude too often that business is very innovative and seizing opportunities, while unwieldy government bodies stand on the sidelines, intervening only when markets fail.

Research by Mariana Mazzucato, Professor of Innovation Economics and Public Value at University College London, has shown that government plays a much bigger role in innovations than is often believed. Take the iPhone as an example. The key technologies for it, such as GPS, the internet, Siri and the touchscreen are all inventions that the government supported. Ditto for 'Generative Pre-trained Transformer', better known as ChatGPT, which uses artificial intelligence. The research and development for this was largely funded by governments.

Without high-risk investments of tax revenues, Apple, Microsoft and Pfizer could never have become so big. Yet many companies, including these multinationals, evade taxes on a global scale even though they make huge profits from government-backed innovation. In effect, the whole society bears the risks of innovation, while the profits go to shareholders and an increasingly small group of wealthy people. This increases inequality and undermines a sustainable and inclusive future.

Hundreds if not thousands of science-based studies show that a sustainable system transition is feasible, affordable and will create jobs. The International Labour Organization (ILO) report, *World Employment and Social Outlook – Trends 2018*, states that a greener economy could create 24 million new jobs globally by 2030. The pioneering report *Net Zero by 2050: A Roadmap for the Global Energy Sector* (2021) by the International Energy Agency (IEA) predicts that an energy transition to clean and renewable sources will create 14 million new jobs related to clean energy technologies and require a shift of about 5 million workers from the fossil fuel sector. In addition to these new jobs, 16 million workers will switch to work in clean energy segments.

Governments are often unaware or insufficiently informed about the innovative and guiding role they can play.

Institutions like the World Bank and the World Economic Forum have the same message; they warn of the destruction of our society and planet. Ignorance is not an excuse; proof that something needs to be done is now well established. It is now time to convert problem analysis into drafting and agreeing on solution-oriented policy.

This is where the shoe pinches: the general framework for both decision making and implementation are unusually complex and time consuming. It can take years to draft, debate, execute, integrate and implement the necessary decisions at the United Nations, the highest decision-making body in the world. The global Development goals, known as Sustainable Development Goals (SDGS), have already been adopted and the Paris Climate Agreement has been voted on.

Earthshot requires speed. At all levels. The only thing blocking the path, the only thing we are lacking is political courage and decisiveness.

COVID as the green flag for Earthshot

Climate and nature do not tolerate us pressing a pause button. History shows that change is possible. How can we precipitate change against a background of complexity?

We can learn a lot by analysing the COVID-19 pandemic.
1. Actions based on scientific analysis were agreed;
2. Actions were codified into policies;
3. International regulators and scientists cooperated to agree on strategies that reduced vaccine development timelines by two thirds;
4. Profound changes in behaviour occurred within an unexpectedly short timeframe, at all levels of society and in government and private organisations;
5. Costs were immediately accepted by governments and seen as an investment in a healthy society;
6. The familiar rationale of feasible and affordable was suddenly replaced by necessary.

In short, the global community – at all levels – immediately did what was necessary.

COVID-19 teaches us that scientific facts are not established by majority vote and that public-only discussion evenings are not the right platform to assess scientific determinations. They are, however, necessary to provide interpretation and open discussion of the science and its implications. The COVID pandemic made it very clear that belief and commitment on the part of stakeholders requires a consistent demonstration of consequences, that change is happening. Effects must happen quickly, and they must be visible and tangibly linked.

Several practical challenges must be met:

1. How can we demonstrate cause and effect in the case of bio-diversity loss and climate change when it can take a long time before the effects of changes are visible?
2. Who should take the initiative? Governments? Companies? International organisations? Local society? Together or separately? Bottom-up or top-down?
3. Transformative public policies are usually fast tracked only in periods of crisis: when the situation is inevitable and unavoidable and the pressure to do nothing becomes untenable. When necessity prevails.
4. How can the benefits of protecting nature be quantified and valued? Companies and investors take initiative and risk based on their own product or service and the prospect of financial stability. Added value creation is possible, but so far largely only as a by-product.
5. Local populations want stability, quality of life and comfort and are quite willing to invest in their family network, local community and in global solidarity. We need to move away from egocentric thinking and think instead, 'Is this good for the community?'. Because what is good for the community is good for everyone, including me. So, more Ubuntu, more 'I am because we are'.

The higher the communal, intrinsic and socio-economic value of protecting the planet and the greater the visible collective connection, the greater the chance of sustainable and nature-rich change. Despite great advances in knowledge, biodiversity and climate change are still often in the losing camp. Yes, we are getting better at fighting the consequences, but we hesitate when it comes to preventing or addressing the causes. We need courage and we need leadership to resolutely launch systemic change and start a sustainable transition.

Now is the time for action, the time to leave analysis behind and move to active action. Time to create the conditions, will and appetite to make a positive turnaround and initiate recovery. Time to show resilience. Glocal (Global plus local) thinking and acting, with the local serving the global goals. Time also to show decisiveness and courage, real leadership from governments, companies and us.

In this first chapter, I have described the danger of the silent death of our planet. The alarm signals that our planet is now sending out are unmistakable and give an indication of the possible consequences of the impact of our western way of life and how fatal it is for building a sustainable future for people and animals. Here and there a light is shining; there are traces of hope. There are leaders who dare to make the choice, there are voters who are persuaded by a narrative committed to survival, and there are enough solid scientific insights to make an Earthshot. If entrepreneurs and government join hands, as all major economic successes are a result of that collaboration, then the solutions are there for the taking. It starts with you, the reader, joining in to make that Earthshot possible. In the following chapters, I dive deeper and deeper into reality, searching for light and solutions. Are there local solutions to global problems and global solutions to local problems? And above all, if we need to change, how do we do it? One thing is certain: 'Nothing is permanent except change.' If change is a constant, we had better learn from it.

Chapter 2

"You can't have unlimited growth on a finite planet."

– former Unilever CEO Paul Polman

BIODIVERSITY, CLIMATE AND AGRICULTURE SOLUTIONS

What exactly are we talking about?

Everyone has heard about the problems of biodiversity, climate change and transforming our industry and agriculture. The terms are complicated and become mixed up when talking about the various problems and possible solutions to the point where the discussion becomes totally confusing. The ecological problems we face here on Earth can be just a complicated and inextricable set of words. We seem to recognise that we face a huge problem but there are so many conflicting opinions and interests; some are well intended while others are driven by not so noble intentions. Our world is polarised into two camps, the winners and the losers. Tragically, if we go on like this, we will all be losers, but we could choose to all be winners.

So, what are we really talking about? What are the facts when we talk about biodiversity and climate change? What exactly do we not yet know and what can we state with 100 per cent certainty? Why is biodiversity so important now for everyone living on this planet and what can we start doing today to turn the tide? How have we become addicted to our western life that seems to exist only if we destroy the climate? What adaptations can we make today to change our world for the better tomorrow? How can we change agricultural practices to benefit the world for people and for farmers.

It all starts with simply getting the facts straight and experiencing with your own eyes and ears what is going on. We are on the road to change and a healthier planet when we all realise that each of us with can make a difference in what our living environments look like.

The Club of Rome released its landmark report *Limits to Growth* in 1972 (see Chapter 1). That was the year I turned eight and understood for the first time that there are limits to what nature can handle. I knew nothing of the Club of Rome, nor about its report and had no sense of what was going on outside my little world in and around Heusden-Zolder, in north-east Belgium. What I did know was that I loved creatures. While romping in the meadow behind my house, I suddenly noticed a beautiful seven-spotted ladybird crawling across the leaf of a bramble bush. When I got too close, the ladybird opened its strange-looking bulbous wings half-way, ready to take off. 'She will be mine', I thought to myself. I ran home and nicked one of my father's matchboxes, tipped out the matches and rushed back to the bramble bush in pursuit of my ladybird. I found her and with my little hand placed her along with a few blades of grass – I thought, 'She has to eat' – in the matchbox. I remember thinking, 'She's mine.' As many as one hundred times a day I opened the matchbox to observe my cherished ladybird. But after just three days, disaster struck. I had to shake the box to see my possession move. My ladybird had died; I cried and cried. I realised that I should not have locked her up.

Looking back at this childhood adventure as a young adult it occurred to me that it was an analogy of what we have done to nature. If you confine a ladybird (= nature) in a box (= reserve), fail to provide it with food and drink (= degraded habitat), exposed to toxic solvent residue from the matches (= poor environmental conditions), allow only occasional extra oxygen and light (= restriction of essential growth factors), in a far too warm pocket (= warming) and allow no contact with other creatures or habitats (= isolation), it dies. I realised that I had assigned the creature to an unnatural habitat and that I had assumed a role that I had no right to take. As a young boy I had to learn that in nature, everything is related to everything else, and nothing can be treated in isolation.

Climate change is detrimental to biodiversity and one of the causes of biodiversity loss. The rate of climate change will increase if biodiversity and ecosystems are not protected. So, climate change and biodiversity are two sides of the same coin. In this chapter I will try to bring clarity to the discussion of biodiversity and climate change. It can be difficult to reconcile the perspectives of economics and ecology when discussing climate change and biodiversity. One loses perspective; the apt expression is that one cannot see the forest for the trees. Arguments for one or the other perspective are only heeded on one's own stage and in one's own bubble. An integrated approach is possible. Agreements and conventions, signed by world leaders can help us all move forward. But of equal and perhaps greater importance is for all of us to reach out to one another to reach sustainable agreements together with governments. There are many examples.

An integrated approach is possible, if all of us reach out to one another to reach sustainable agreements together with governments.

Biodiversity, where everything is connected to everything else

Let me start with a story from my life to illustrate connectedness. I learned an important lesson as a little boy in the environmentally conscious seventies. Nature, all life, should not be separated or isolated, it should be free and connected. What applied to the ladybird in the matchbox applies even more to us. Without protest we are becoming like the ladybird, locked in and isolated in an ever-shrinking polluted box. We are an inseparable part of nature. It is time that we realise and internalise this.

Survival is – quite literally – in our nature. But who saves whom? Do we save nature or does nature save us? The more I learn about nature and from nature, the more convinced I become that nature will save us if we give it the chance. Great power lies in restoring our connections with nature, from intertwining with it. You are invited to join me on an exploration into the wonderful world of nature in this chapter. What exactly is the role of biodiversity and what exactly is the relationship between biodiversity and the climate? What are the effects on agriculture and what can we do about this? How can we protect biodiversity and the climate in an integrated and inclusive way, collectively on a global level, locally with friends and beginning with you?

Biodiversity as the silent foundation of our existence

My first-hand appreciation of the concept of biodiversity, began in June 1993, when a dozen West Flanders conservationists visited the Belgian province of Limburg to find out more about the design and success of the Limburg Ponds plan. At that time, the province had already been at the forefront of Flemish nature policy for several years. Forty percent of Flemish nature and 90% of all species found in Flanders are observed in Limburg. The Ponds plan was undertaken to strengthen the viability and distribution of amphibian populations. It involved the restoration of old dry ponds and the creation of new ponds.

The Ponds plan set me on a voyage of discovery into the realm of biodiversity. A leading character in the story of my voyage was played by a special toad that encouraged me to knock on the door of the authorities; to make a difference on behalf of nature. Allow me to take you along for that story.

Biodiversity is a word that is bandied about and has a slightly different meaning depending on who is doing the talking. Some view biodiversity as a concern for biologists and other specialists, when in fact it is a topic that concerns us all and should receive our full attention every day starting today. Biodiversity concerns the variety of life in an area, from a leaf stem to an entire forest to all the Earth. Biodiversity includes all species of plants, animals and microorganisms, the enormous genetic variation within them and the variety of ecosystems they are a part of, from swamps to deserts, mountains to oceans, ice flows to meadows; everywhere. So, it is far from just about flowers, trees and cuddly animals. The term encompasses the total package of living organisms and systems, and the interactions between them. Biodiversity is also about nature constantly adapting to the space we give it and proving itself extraordinarily resilient again and again. We just need to give nature the space back to restore itself and help us again. My own story is a great example of this.

Let me start at the beginning. Booted and armed with binoculars and aquatic sampling nets, my friend Dirk Bauwens and I guided the conservationists through the hilly Haspengouw region of southern Limburg, sharing our expertise on construction and restoration at each pond and the species to be found there. Dirk is a top scientist and an internationally renowned authority at the Institute for Nature and Forest Research (INBO).

Something extraordinary suddenly happened on that day, an experience that biologists dream of. We arrived at a small, ancient meadow pond fed by clear spring water. Intervals of strange short, high-pitched whistles resounded over the water. A rush of adrenaline shot through my body as I thought, 'What is that?' The sound was not coming from the pond, but rather from the ground. I got down on my hands and knees and crawled around near the pond, pausing every few metres to cup my hands behind my ears to magnify the sound, eager to discover the owner of this bizarre whistle. I was so astonished by the sound that I kept looking at the group to see if anyone might be playing a prank. I moved carefully towards the sound and when I thought I had located the spot, I pushed back a handful of grass and, lo and behold, a small, brownish-grey toad was hiding there. It was if the creature had leaped straight out of a David Attenborough documentary. There was a string of golden-yellow eggs wrapped around its hind legs. 'A midwife toad!' I exclaimed (*Alytes obstetricans*).

I knew the species only from literature and had heard the whistle of a midwife toad once whilst on a holiday in France, but I had never seen a midwife toad in person. Still fuelled by adrenaline, I wanted to know everything about the toad, which is rare in Flanders. I whispered to my friend Dirk to carry on with the group while I stayed behind to follow the little thing, thinking that I might find others. It was a breath-taking afternoon and night that I will never forget. That toad was perhaps the reason for my strong commitment to nature conservation in my future life.

The story continued. A hill lay close to the meadow where I discovered the toad, its summit adorned by a small 13th century church that had been rebuilt in later centuries. About 40 mostly ancient headstones marked the graves in an adjacent graveyard. On one of the graves lay the iron helmet of a young soldier, killed early in World War II. The hollows in the cracks and crevices of the church and under the crooked headstones were the ideal habitat for the heat-loving midwife toads. In 1993, this spot was still relatively unknown to conservationists. The midwife toads felt at home there in the south-facing spot, warmed by the rays of the evening sun. Life and death were united there in the man-made stony environment.

Most amphibians mate in water but the midwife toad mates on land. The males call, or rather whistle, to entice the females to join them in their warm burrows, which in this case were the dark crevices of the church. The old gravestones amplified the sound, especially in the evening when the whistling males came out of their burrows to show themselves to the willing ladies.

Men whistling at ladies seems to transcend all ages and all species. When a willing female shows interest and presents herself, the male pounces on her and, via a complicated midwife toad-Kama Sutra pose involving a hip mating grip and a head mating grip – for the experts among us – then proceeding with the birthing procedure. Once the male is firmly in place, he massages the female's abdomen with his front legs until she signals that she is about to give birth to her eggs, which are connected by an egg cord. Ingeniously and quickly, the male and female toads make a bowl with their hind legs, allowing the male to fertilise the eggs externally and immediately in the bowl. The male thus helps the female give birth, so to speak. This explains the toad's name. As the final part of mating, the male wraps the fertilised egg string around his hind legs. For the next forty days, the male will take care of the toad larvae, which can grow on without much worry. Eventually, the hefty larvae reach a stage when they are better armed against predators, and they will be neatly deposited by dad in the water to grow into adults.

Again, the story continued. A few years later, stabilisation problems were identified in the little church and attempts were made
to repair its sagging and cracking walls. Another issue was that
lack of space had put pressure on the small graveyard. The town
council decided to remove the graves of people for which there
were no living relatives. A newsletter announced that all graves
that were not visited on All Saints' Day would be cleared.

The entire habitat of my toads was in peril; their doomsday
was imminent. Could it be any more symbolic? I had to quickly
come up with something to save time. I decided to strike up a
conversation with the mayor to convince him of the presence and
interesting symbiosis of these rare midwife toads: A challenging
task for a passionate naturalist to convince a rational administra-
tor. Previous attempts had so far ended in failure, so I devised a
second strategy. I bought so many flowers on the eve of All Saints'
Day that I had enough for every old and unvisited grave. I made
floral tributes to people I did not know, trying to offer a last chance
of life to toads so close to my heart. My personal act of heroism
paid off. Fourteen days later, I was granted the chance to meet with
the mayor and miraculously managed to convince him of the need
to protect the toads' habitat. I advised on the stabilisation of the
little church and the gravestones remained in place. Operation
Alytes obstetricans succeeded. A humble little example of how, by
being a little creative, you can connect with nature. You can be
courageous.

Several years ago, a decision was made to compile a distribution atlas of amphibians and reptiles in Belgium's Limburg province. A network of volunteers was assembled to search unique
places and other likely habitats selected by specialist researchers.
I was one of them and was responsible for drafting the distribution
atlas. I spent almost every night over several years happily on the
trail of the creatures. Armed with traps, a sampling net, boots, a
neoprene suit, a headlamp and a notebook, I dove into the night
and the water, occasionally getting lost, both literally and figuratively. In the process I marvelled each time I heard a tree frog or
natterjack toad concert. After several years of data collection,

I could finally start writing the distribution atlas. My conclusion was that between 1975 and 1994, Limburg had 11 species of frogs and toads and four species of reptiles. Analysis of the data showed that banality was increasing, meaning that common species were becoming more common and rare species more rare. Such developments are seen with increasing frequency worldwide.

Recreationists walking or cycling through the countryside breath in the fresh air and enjoy the surrounding greenery, unaware that they may be strolling through an area that is gradually becoming a disaster zone. Indeed, I was not the only one who noticed this during my distribution atlas tours. Fellow researchers, working with birds, plants and mammals, also came up with a similar, disturbing conclusion: nature is collapsing. Existing nature is disappearing because of agricultural intensification and the construction of housing estates and business and industrial parks. The natural and qualitative landscape is being stripped, including the natural infrastructure: small landscape elements such as hedges, hedge-rows, ditches and ponds are disappearing from the landscape at an astonishing rate. Unspoiled land links between natural areas are disappearing, rapidly reducing connectivity. It is like the streets to your village and home are disappearing, abruptly severing contact with family, neighbours and others. Communities are becoming isolated as a result and can no longer exchange with other populations; some collapse and threaten to disappear altogether.

Without premeditation, my colleagues and I had, in a way, relived my experiences with my seven-spotted ladybird. We had again uncovered several elements underlying species disappearance. Isolation of parts of nature, habitat disruption and habitat loss are endangering biodiversity and, little by little, destabilising our existence. My work on the distribution atlas caused a storm in my mind that raged ever more frequently. I found myself pondering the question: How can we turn the tide? How can we protect our nature from the ticking time bomb? How can we ensure that nature will survive us, regardless of its appearance, or size, regardless of its distance and time? Surely my colleagues and I were not the only ones aware of the problem? Were the same phenomena taking place elsewhere, and have others found a way to call attention to this, but also to do something about it?

How everything in nature is related to everything else

I will give you an example to explain to you how resilient nature can be. For example, in the country of Mozambique, you can see Darwin's principles at work on a daily basis. The persistent hunting of ivory over the past hundred years has had a severe negative pressure on elephant populations. Elephants without tusks have been ignored by poachers and their offspring have had an evolutionary advantage. Research shows that the number of elephants born with tusks has decreased and the converse is true. Elephants have miraculously managed to adapt and improved their chances for survival.

What is true for a ladybird, for midwife toads and for elephants is true for all of nature, as biologists will tell you. Just as creatures are not alone in the world, neither are we humans; everything in nature relates to everything else. It is disastrous to think that we can solve climate change and biodiversity problems in isolation. More and more humans taking up more and more space are putting more and more habitats and more and more species at risk. More than one million species are threatened with extinction by the end of this century. Sometimes we manage to (temporarily) prevent extinction in a certain species, but these are exceptions. Species must constantly adapt to survive, but if conditions change and the ability to adapt proves insufficient, they irrevocably disappear. Sometimes species fall into an ecological trap and not infrequently we make decisions that cause the loss of a species. It is a constant survival of the fittest: adapt or disappear.

Another example of the ingenuity of nature is the wonderous phenomenon of plants and trees communicating with each other through the *wood wide web*, a network of fungal threads. Fungi make up about half of the living organisms in our soils.

Just as creatures are not alone in the world, neither are we humans. It is disastrous to think that we can solve climate change and biodiversity problems in isolation.

Most fungi lead an existence invisible to humans, but some bear fruit in the form of mushrooms, just like an apple on a tree. Scientists recently discovered that right under our feet, billions of kilometres of fungal networks snake through the soil. Those networks store carbon underground, communicate with each other and transport water and nutrients along the planet's underground ecosystems.

You can clearly see how plants and fungus communicate with each other in the example of shield acacia trees in Africa. The leaves of acacias *(Acacia sieberiana)* are a delicacy for giraffes, and the animals can quickly devour almost all the acacia with their long necks. Although the trees are quite resilient, regular scalping can kill them. The trees protect themselves from being denuded of all their leaves by producing and sending toxins to their leaves. The toxin accumulates in leaf buds making them taste bad to the giraffes and the toxin is lethal if consumed in sufficient quantities. The toxins are converted into a gas that travels through the air to neighbouring acacia, alerting them produce the toxin. The giraffes, in turn, have adapted by starting feasting on trees downwind from other acacias because communication between trees against the wind is somewhat slower, increasing the time needed for the formation of the toxic leaves.

The story of the dodo is a sad symbol that nature's resilience can be finite. The dodo, perhaps the most famous of birds, lived in the forests of Mauritius and became extinct between 1680 and 1690. This plump is repeated further along bird, a distant cousin of the pigeon, was one metre tall, plump, with a large beak, and had lost its ability to fly. Dodos had no natural predators. Until humans arrived. Dutch settlers arrived in Mauritius with rats and pigs which wreaked havoc by eating the dodo eggs and young dodos, drove the dodo into extinction. Since then, the dodo has been a symbol of the disappearance of species due to the degradation of nature by human activity.

Other examples of how things go wrong is when animals misjudge where to breed. Sometimes species fall into an ecological trap because they are seduced by the attraction of unsuitable habitats. Think, for example, of a lapwing or skylark that wants to breed in arable land or grassland that is ploughed up or mowed before its young can escape. Or think of dragonflies that want to deposit eggs on a polished granite tombstone because they perceive the same brilliance as water there. The animals think they have found a suitable habitat, but they walk, fly and jump into a deadly ecological trap.

But mostly it is humans themselves who make ill-considered decisions. Take the disaster that occurred in New Zealand around 1860. New residents introduced rabbits to the island as a familiar way to provide for sport, meat, and clothes made from their pelts. But the proliferation capability of rabbits was not considered. Rabbits soon escaped and multiplied like ... rabbits, and became an outright plague. Ferrets, ermine and weasels – martens – were introduced to combat the rabbit plague and were protected by law in 1880. The martens, also new to New Zealand, had no natural predators and adapted very well. They found it much easier to gobble up native species than to chase the speedy rabbits. So, the consequence has ultimately been that the martens have posed a threat to native species. Despite all the good intentions of humans, marten-related disasters have continued to occur to this day. The current government wants to eradicate all feral predators by 2050. Time will tell if this set of good intentions will succeed. Human intervention in ecological systems rarely proves successful.

Man is a creature prone to ill-considered initiatives. Take the example of the escapee frogs. The American bullfrog, prized for their hefty legs, was imported into Europe from North America beginning in the 1930s. This species, too, soon managed to escape from farms and adapted well to the European climate. They consumed almost everything in their path, from amphibians and birds to small mammals, as they hopped across the continent. Since the 1930s, the American bullfrog has taken over half of Europe and poses a serious threat to native species. Invasive plant and animal species are becoming more numerous, and we will have to come up with multiple responses for these newcomers. Nature turns out to be powerful, inventive and resilient, but when we humans make ill-considered interventions, we are certainly not helping nature nor ourselves. So, time to change tack.

Nature is becoming increasingly less able to take corrective action in response to man's actions. What is the impact of human interventions in nature and how do species respond to new situations?

The most important thing to know is that changing conditions lead to changing situations. With the Anthropocene, we have entered a very dangerous situation with constant and, especially, very rapidly changing conditions. Species are literally and figuratively pushed to the limit to survive in an unstable climate. Sometimes species manage to survive by adapting quickly. Frequently the opposite occurs; they are unable to adapt and become extinct. Gone. Forever. It is up to us humans to come up with solutions. Solutions can often be found in being more connected and cooperative, both globally and in our small, local biotope.

Pigeonholing is not a solution

Parties must come together and reach agreements to tackle global climate and biodiversity problems. The responsibility to find solutions and make decisions is frequently divided amongst different groups. This is a mistake because if you solve a problem on one side, it can go horribly wrong on another. We must not tackle problems in isolation and fail to see that everything in the world is connected to everything else and requires an integrated and inclusive approach. If we take an inclusive approach, nature will respond directly and cooperate in the solution.

Luckily, the negative evolution us conservationists are witnessing can be addressed on a global scale. The United Nations, for example, was founded in 1945 with the aim of preventing war in the future at any cost. Almost every country in the world is a member. Agreements are made to organise and implement well-defined goals worldwide and codified in treaties and conventions. World peace is a common concern, but members are also concerned about the health of our living environment. We make global agreements on that too. Conventions on climate (UNFCCC) and nature (UNCBD), for instance, and the Sustainable Development Goals (SDGs) have been agreed on by members. At the 1992 Rio de Janeiro Earth Summit, the Convention on Biological Diversity (CBD) was born, with the major goal of protecting biological and genetic diversity. Regarding strategic agreements with nature, targets have been agreed every decade. The last CBD Nature Summit – COP 15 – concluded in December 2022 in

Montreal, Canada with a landmark agreement to guide global action on nature until 2030. This new Global Biodiversity Framework (GBF) – aims to address biodiversity loss, restore ecosystems and protect the rights of indigenous peoples. The plan includes concrete measures to halt and reverse the loss of nature, including putting 30% of the planet and 30% of degraded ecosystems (land and water) under protection by 2030, and increases funding for developing countries.

While making commitments and signing agreements on a global scale may be necessary and raise awareness of nature dependency, implementing them has proven to be complex and difficult. It is not so easy for sovereign countries (member states) to think, act and cooperate in a global context. Because international treaties sometimes have opposite goals, economics and ecology come into competition with each other, with ecological arguments often losing out. Despite our good intentions, why do we fail to solve the common problems we have with conservation? Why do we fail to resolve the contradictions between economics and ecology?

Good intentions are laudable, but issues that are related and should be treated together are separated and treated independently.

To address the question of how to make agreements between sovereign countries: people think they can act much more efficiently in policy terms if they separate functions, objectives and tasks by region. But alas, as the story of the ladybird teaches us, separating and isolating leads to undesirable results. When major political and economic interests are at stake, this often means separating agriculture from nature. By not bringing economic and ecological interests together, we ensure that we do not address the underlying issues, thereby exacerbating the problems. We seem to forget that there is much more that binds the two sectors together than separates them. The solution lies in bringing these worlds together.

The intentions are good, and the enthusiasm, activism and managerial commitment are laudable. But in local and global approaches, we keep walking with open eyes into the pitfalls we have dug for ourselves. Increasingly Protecting areas here and there in the absence of coordinated standards and protocols is like taking water to the sea. We must have an integrated approach.

we realise that we are sawing off the branch on which we ourselves sit. By destroying nature, we are destroying ourselves. The scientific evidence for the collapse of natural ecosystems is abundantly clear. I repeat this point; the most authoritative reports are irrefutable.

The Global Assessment Report on Biodiversity and Ecosystem Services by the Inter-Governmental Science-Policy Platform on Biodiversity and Ecosystem Services (IPBES) is the most comprehensive study conducted worldwide to date. It shows that one million species are threatened with extinction in the coming decades. It is a similar story to that of the World Wildlife Fund's (WWF) latest *Living Planet Index* report. This index measures trends in thousands of populations of mammals, birds, reptiles, amphibians and fish around the world and shows declines averaging 68 per cent since 1970. Every report, whether national, European or global, shows the same alarming trend.

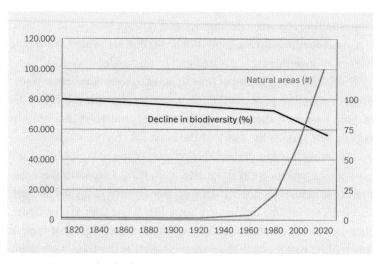

FIGURE: *The evolution in biodiversity and protected natural areas in Europe*
SOURCE: Based on figures from EEA – *Protected Areas in Europe* (2012) and EEA – *Data – Nationally Designated Areas* (CDDA) (2021)

It is also abundantly clear that economics and ecology must not be treated as separate issues. Consider, for instance, a report by the authoritative European Environment Agency (EEA) examining the number of government-designated nature conservation areas in Europe in the period 1838-2009. It paints a positive story, and at the same time a very negative one. Allow me to explain.

The history of wanting to simultaneously protect economic interests and care for nature is an example of what can go wrong when economics and ecology are treated as separate issues, in two separate cubicles. This graph shows that until the 1960s, few or no protected natural areas were designated by European governments. From the 1970s onwards – a period that began with an international awakening to the importance of environmental causes – the number of designated nature conservation areas grew exponentially. The data reflects the power of society to influence political policy. The voice of society was heard, and politicians responded.

However, planning to designate and establish protected nature reserves is only a first step. If the designations are not followed up, there is no guarantee of biodiversity conservation and restoration. Protecting areas here and there in the absence of coordinated standards and protocols is like taking water to the sea. We must have an integrated approach. Planning protection is only effective if there is enforcement as well as adequate management and restoration in addition to a legislative legal initiative. Only then can you guarantee the conservation of species and habitats.

In Europe, too, there are several initiatives that demonstrate that the loss of biodiversity has been taken seriously and that aim to restore the balance. The exponential increase in the number of designated nature conservation areas and the demand for additional measures was also strongly influenced by European Union initiatives from the 1970s onwards. At that time, policy preparation in the European Union was still prepared from a scientific approach. Brussels was literally and figuratively still too far away, and European policy initiatives for nature did not pose a threat to domestic policy. With relatively little effort, the largest policy network for nature in the world could be built. These so-called Natura 2000 sites are composed of the EU Birds Directive (1979) and the EU Habitats Directive (1992) requiring EU member states to designate and protect Europe's top nature – species and habitats of Community interest – as Natura 2000 sites.

But as is so often the case, all is not what it seems: the increased political attention and exponential growth of designated nature sites could not prevent a significant decline in biodiversity over the same period. It is a kind of nature paradox, where biodiversity was inversely proportional to the exponential growth of protected natural areas over the same period. The reason for the paradox is sobering, but also easy to explain. Over the decades – and under the guise of economic growth – nature was separated from other functions, no longer approached holistically, then neatly 'locked up' in protected nature reserves. Another example of pigeonholing, in other words.

Without fully realising it, pigeonholing and a desire not to impede economic growth has severed our connection with nature. Nature reserves have evolved into isolated islands in a barren and ossified sea, as though nature has been banned or outlawed outside of protected areas. Other functions such as the intensification of agriculture, urbanisation and industrial development were regarded as superordinate functions, because of which both the intrinsic and multifunctional value of nature rapidly declined. As a result, environmental pressures from outside increased, often greatly reducing the size and quality of habitats in designated nature reserves, and species with very specific requirements were weakened and/or disappeared.

Consider, for example, the negative impact of acidification, eutrophication, disturbance and poisoning (pesticides) or the nitrogen issue on habitats. Habitats that were unlucky not to be designated as protected areas disappeared like snow in the sun. Connectivity and genetic exchange between species weakened sharply or simply became impossible. Result: the pernicious collapse of biodiversity and natural ecosystems. It is an excoriating picture of how we have treated nature in recent decades.

Natural resilience outside the boxes

However much we humans screw up, nature always has surprising solutions to the problems we have created. Fortunately, the collapse of biodiversity has not yet occurred completely and everywhere. Fortunately, there are still points of light, pilot lights, that can be quickly reignited. Nature has developed a kind of built-in resilience to survive extreme conditions through millions of years of evolution. Trapped species of plants and animals in isolated nature reserves can sometimes survive for long periods of time, with the principle being that the larger the protected nature reserve is, the better the chances of survival for the species found in it. This principle is based on 'island theory', which links the biodiversity of an island to the combination of its surface area, climatic conditions and its distance from the mainland.

Efforts to protect and restore nature often lead to surprisingly positive results. Some species can quickly build stable populations and spread rapidly when conditions are improved. However much we humans screw up, nature always has surprising solutions to the problems we have created. Another bright spot: the number of species of plants and animals is usually higher in protected nature areas, the decline of populations there is slower and can sometimes be reversed with very positive results. Species can then build stable populations and spread if conditions – such as, for example, the size of the space allocated to nature – improve. That is why it is so enormously important that national and international organisations such as IUCN, WWF, Sierra Club, Rewilding Europe, Rewilding Argentina, Forgotten Parks Foundation, EUROPARC Federation, (and – in Belgium and the Netherlands – Natuurpunt, Natuurmonumenten, Limburgs Landschap, ...) can continue to develop to their full potential and remain committed to nature conservation and protection. Through their work and commitment, opportunities for nature and species recovery remain real. Through their efforts, nature reserves can start to expand again, and conditions are created to allow nature to regain its self-direction through, among other things, the (re)introduction of large grazers. Since thousands of plant and animal species depend directly or indirectly on large grazers and have evolved with natural grazing, (re-)introducing large grazers improves living conditions for thousands of other organisms.

I am repeatedly surprised by the resilience of nature. European carnivores are a good example. Due mainly to the scaling-up of agriculture and industry in the nineteenth and early twentieth centuries, wolves, bears, lynxes and wolverines reached their lowest point. People at that time had nothing to do with these majestic top predators. Until the 1960s, the Spanish government even paid bounties for killing Iberian wolves and lynxes. The convincing power and evidence of the ever-stronger wildlife organisations changed public opinion on wildlife conservation. Public pressure ensured the success of a political initiative. Together with Monaco, Burkina Faso, Morocco, Tunisia and Senegal, the European Council adopted the Bern Convention in 1979. Later, the contents of this treaty were fully incorporated into European Birds and Habitats legislation. This international treaty protects wild animal and plant species as well as their habitats. Bears, wolves, lynxes and wolverines received legal protection. Thanks to the efforts of organisations such as Rewilding Europe, many successful rewilding projects were set up, resulting in the spectacular recovery of some populations. Meanwhile, wolves have repopulated parts of Scandinavia, Finland, France, Switzerland, Germany, Belgium and the Netherlands, bears have been reintroduced to Austria and a small number of bears have been moved from Slovenia to the French Pyrenees and the Italian Alps. Lynx have returned to their historic range. The animals are accepting their protection with thanks and are showing tremendous resilience: the number of European carnivores is increasing and was estimated to be around 17,000 brown bears, 12,000 wolves, 9,000 Eurasian lynxes and 1,200 wolverines in 2018.

New success stories are also being written outside Europe. In Argentina, for example, jaguars and giant river otter are getting plenty of new chances for survival thanks to the efforts of Rewilding Argentina, and thanks to the efforts of the Snow Leopard Trust, snow leopards have better chances for survival in Kyrgyzstan. The protection and recovery of rhinoceros populations in Africa and Asia is being realised by the 'International Rhino Foundation', the fantastic work of Virunga National Park in protecting mountain gorillas and the Jane Goodall Institute's commitment to protecting chimpanzees are unprecedented.

In the right circumstances, the resilience of nature and its living organisms is extraordinary, sometimes even spectacular. It shows that protecting and restoring natural ecosystems can be successful and that international cooperation and regulation pay off. Nevertheless, we must not be blind to the still rapid decline in biodiversity, and we must not be deaf to news of continued natural destruction. There are bright spots; awareness that we cannot do without nature is growing and there is more openness to a nature-inclusive society. Hopefully, this will give more and better opportunities in the future to the methodologies and models that will enable the protection and restoration of our natural ecosystems while tackling the new sustainability challenges of our society.

The observation that politicians respond to societal pressure is important to consider in the preparation and development of new models of change. Building sufficient public and political support can stimulate and accelerate a change process and is often a decisive argument for change. But by no means will all decisions taken be popular or receive strong public support. Think of extra taxes, for which there is rarely public support. Sometimes decisions come first, and support must be recruited afterwards. This was the case with many COVID-related measures. On the other hand, the absence of sufficient support is often invoked by politicians and used as an argument for inaction. I have to repeat it: right decisions don't become wrong decisions when everyone is against them, and wrong decisions are not right decisions when there is a lot of support for them. And even a right decision taken too late is often a wrong decision. In any case, it is up to us to help nature restore itself.

Taking natural resilience into account

I talked about pigeonholing above and about how nature is becoming trapped in nature reserves and about nature's resilience. We need to be aware of two things: that the clock is ticking, and that nature's resilience is finite.

Clearly, we are currently in the sixth wave of extinction with species of plants and animals dying out up to a thousand times faster than in pre-human times. Could it really be different in any way? The late Edward Osborne Wilson, one of the world's greatest natural scientists and thinkers, had some ideas on that. I had the pleasure of speaking with him twice, once in Jeju (South Korea) and once in Hawaii, and each time I was impressed by his calm and open demeanour. Wilson was a world authority on biodiversity and biogeography and one of the founders of sociobiology, the biological basis of social behaviour. In his long scientific career, he conducted research mainly on ants, of which he alone described more than 400 new species.

It was Wilson's belief that we have reached the end game in the 21st century. 'It's win or lose', he told me. 'If we do not quickly realise our dependence on healthy natural ecosystems, we will lose momentum and face uncontrollable and irreversible destructive developments. We will need to protect half of the planet's natural ecosystems to preserve 80% of all living organisms on earth.' In his fantastic book *Half Earth*, he explains that this goal remains possible if we make the right choices. With the explosive growth of technology in recent decades, the intensity and importance of employing so-called bnr technologies, (biotechnology, nanotechnology and robotics) in the global economy has grown. This is where Wilson saw opportunities. He believed that these technologies have the potential to both destroy and protect nature. Wilson wanted to believe that we will come to the right realisation before it is too late. Protecting and restoring our natural ecosystems, phasing out our fossil fuel addiction and radically changing our eating patterns and food production systems are crucial to this. After conversations like the ones I had with Wilson, I feel especially grateful and my head buzzes with ideas. Surely there must be a way to turn the tide. I feel I am getting closer and closer to finding a solution.

Scientific knowledge shows that since the creation of our planet, new species keep appearing and disappearing. Moreover, the fossil record shows that there have been five mass extinction events when significant numbers of the earth's species became extinct due to catastrophic changes to the climate. Past events were the result of major geological phenomena such as meteorite impacts or volcanic eruptions that changed the climate to the point where many species could not survive. These extinction events occurred over thousands to millions of years. Scientists agree that we are now in the sixth extinction wave; that it is being caused by humans; and that it is taking place over a few decades. Our unsustainable use of land, water and energy is having a devastating effect on the health of our living environment (see Chapter 1) and posing a danger for all living organisms, including ourselves and the tree frog (see the Introduction).

The absence of spectacular climatic fluctuations or extremes over the last tens of thousands of years allowed humans to build a more or less stable society. Unfortunately, we did so without considering the consequences that are now rapidly disrupting our comfortable and stable position. Climate and nature are intimately linked. Writing about biodiversity without discussing its inseparable relationship with climate change is not possible, nor desirable, and could also misdirect our search for solutions. We must not forget that biodiversity and climate change are two sides of the same coin.

Climate, the biggest task

The climate concerns us all

Doing something about the climate and working on the problem of biodiversity is often thought of as a role for big players on the world stage. I realised after I met Al Gore at a conference in San Francisco that it is also something for a humble Belgian like me. Gore, former US VP during Clinton's presidency, who lost the presidency to George W Bush by a hair in 2000, has experience in how geopolitics works. He has a long-term commitment to preventing the dangerous consequences of climate change. Gore released his documentary film *An Inconvenient Truth* in 2006. In retrospect, without realising it, Gore's activism may have exacerbated the politicisation of the climate issue back then. I met with Gore in a private room at San Francisco's beautiful and stately Opera House in 2009, just before the presentation of the Goldman Environmental Prize. I had received this prize, the world's highest prize for champions of environmental causes, also called the green Nobel Prize, the year before in 2008. Gore was to give the keynote presentation at the ceremony following our meeting. I was stiff with nerves, having never met someone who had operated at his level in politics. We had about 15 minutes to exchange views.

After my faltering introduction about my work on the nature issue in Europe, I asked why the US had not yet joined the UN climate coalition. Gore replied, 'America wants to become China for one day', a surprising answer for an American. He assured me that Barack Obama, President at that time, and the Democrats wanted to join the UN climate accord but that the political situation, with Republicans holding a majority in the US Senate, made it impossible for them to join the coalition. The former US vice president had told me that the US would like to be China for one day, decide by diktat to join the accord, then quickly revert to being America. My fifteen minutes with Gore were special and informative. I realised that it is possible to have a pleasant and normal conversation with a world leader and that the problems we face are essentially the same everywhere whether one lives in America, the Netherlands, Belgium or anywhere. I had to admit, there was little enthusiasm for the UN climate agreement amongst people in my immediate community either. Gore concluded our conversation by saying, 'Let's stay in touch.' Only a pleasantry, perhaps, but nonetheless, I floated through the evening.

Gore's parting phrase was not a pleasantry after all. In 2012, the world-renowned climate advocate invited me to join his Climate Reality Project. I attended a training course in Istanbul in 2013 along with several hundred other climate warriors from all over the world, and again Gore asked to have a short face-to-face talk. I felt a tiny bit special. Gore wanted to coordinate US and European leadership, with me driving the agenda for climate issues in Europe; and Europe sharing leadership with the US to drive the agenda for sustainability. As we talked, I realised that with Clinton's 'It's the economy stupid', Gore had climbed to the role of Vice President in 1993, but 2012 was no different: many leaders, including those in Europe, were still clinging to the idea that everything was about growing the economy and the jobs-jobs-jobs credo. Gore's hopes were partially fulfilled when in 2020 European Commission President Ursula von der Leyen pulled out all the sustainability stops with the Green Deal. In the United States, in contrast, led at the time by President Donald Trump, there was doom and gloom: all previous nature and climate initiatives were scaled down.

Saving the climate is not something we can leave only to world leaders. For us citizens, there is also work to be done.

Saving the climate is not something we can leave only to world leaders. For us citizens, there is also work to be done, and our work is one that must be done before world leaders can make things happen on the global stage. I learned this at the Climate Reality Project training in Istanbul. The training took place at a hotel near Taksim Square. At the same time, a peaceful protest began in Gezi Park that leads off from the square, against the felling of trees and the planned demolition of the park. I was fascinated by the openness and solidarity that prevailed. Thousands of people kept vigil in the park day and night. Residents from the city provided supplies. There was food and drink for everyone, and a makeshift library and pharmacy had been built in the camp. Every evening at seven o'clock, thousands of Turkish women threw open their windows and doors and beat out rhythms of protest with wooden spoons on cooking pots and pans – I do not think I will ever forget the sound. The mood of the protest eventually turned grim. Orders were given to disperse the crowds and at that point Al Gore was evacuated by security forces, even before the training course had ended.

The uncomfortable truth about greenhouse gases

What are we talking about when we talk about the climate? Let me start by explaining the difference between weather and climate and the difference between an occasional nice summer and global warming.

Climate change is caused by a group of gases in the atmosphere that together are referred to as 'greenhouse gases' (GHGS) that have a warming effect on our earth. The atmosphere is a relatively thin layer of gases that encircle the planet and consists of several layers. The main layers are the troposphere, stratosphere, mesosphere, thermosphere and exosphere. Gases of natural origin and gases from industrial sources are found in these layers. The greenhouse gases are carbon dioxide (CO_2), the main greenhouse gas, used as the reference unit, hydrogen (H_2), methane (CH_4), nitrous oxide or laughing gas (N_2O) and ozone (O_3). Industrial greenhouse gases are fluorinated hydrocarbons (CFCS, HCFCS, HFCS, PFCS) among others used for refrigerants and solvents, sulphur hexafluoride (SF_6), and nitrogen trifluoride (NF_3).

What problems are caused by these gases? The term greenhouse gas is an apt generic term because some greenhouse gases have a similar function in the atmosphere as glass does in a greenhouse or conservatory: they trap the sun's heat, preventing it from escaping into space. This is also the main feature of climate change. Greenhouse gases form a kind of insulating blanket that traps the sun's rays. The more greenhouse gases there are in the atmosphere, the more heat is retained under the blanket of gas. This activates a self-reinforcing effect of global warming. Carbon dioxide or CO_2 is considered the most important greenhouse gas because it produces most of the warming effect and it is the greenhouse gas produced most by humans (from fossil fuels and cement production). This also means that we humans can control the production of CO_2 and, thus, its effect on global warming. This is a case where we can sit at the controls, in a sense, of our planet's future. Just imagine if planet Earth was hurtling towards the sun, or if a giant comet was about to collide with Earth as in the film *Don't Look Up*; we would be helpless. But we can control the release of CO_2.

The use of fossil fuels such as oil and gas has exploded. According to NASA, it has doubled the amount of atmospheric CO_2 since the start of the Industrial Revolution in 1750. Other greenhouse gases are fortunately much less prevalent. Yet they are no less dangerous, because some greenhouse gases have a much greater (global) warming potential. Their warming potential is compared to the warming potential of 1 kilogram of CO_2 in a hundred years and is expressed in GWP (Global Warming Potential). For example, the warming potential of methane (CH_4) has 25 times and nitrous oxide (N_2O) has 298 times the CO_2 levels.

Climate change is assessed based on average temperatures, average precipitation and average wind speeds over a 30-year period. Scientists rely on these data to deduce the causes of trends shown by the data and model the likelihood of climate change. This is a totally different exercise than predicting today's weather or a 10-day forecast. An isolated warm summer month does not in itself produce climate change. Climate change describes structural changes to a region's weather. You have seen evidence in the news or may have experienced it first-hand, so you probably do not need to be convinced. There is essentially 100% scientific evidence that global warming is taking place now and that it is caused by humans.

Science has made great strides in recent decades. We can measure greenhouse gases with great certainty. Not only across the planet, but also over time. We can now measure how values vary by area and how they have evolved over the past million years and since the more recent Industrial Revolution with great accuracy. Scientists can measure the constituents of atmospheric air composed of nitrogen, oxygen, argon, and carbon dioxide, with great accuracy and certainty. Their proportion is expressed in the number of parts per million (ppm). The rate at which our earth is warming is mainly determined by the concentration of CO_2 in the atmosphere. CO_2 is the most important greenhouse gas, and its atmospheric level is therefore closely monitored.

Since the 1950s, the concentration of CO_2, among other things, has been measured at the Mauna Loa Observatory in Hawaii, a world-renowned research station with authoritative status. Its location and low levels of pollution in the local atmospheric layers make the measurements very reliable. CO_2 concentrations can be tracked by the public on the Global Monitoring Laboratory's website. On 2 June 2023, the CO_2 concentration was 424.58 ppm, an increase of 2.94 ppm (0.70%) from a year ago. The data are clear and shown on the following graph: since the 1960s, CO_2 concentration has risen from some 350 ppm to 424.58 ppm in June 2023. Climate scientists calculate that the CO_2 value should be below 350 ppm to stay below a maximum warming of 1.5°C.

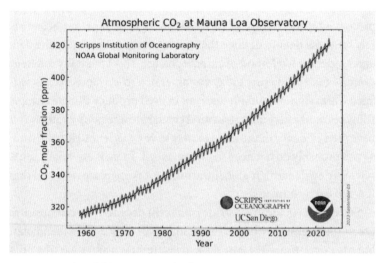

FIGURE: *the rise of CO2 concentration in the atmosphere*
SOURCE: Mauna Loa Observatory, Global Monitoring Laboratory (2023)

In 2016, I was in Hawaii as president of EUROPARC Federation for the World Congress of the International Union for the Conservation of Nature (IUCN). Awareness of rapidly collapsing natural ecosystems, biodiversity loss and climate change were high on the agenda of the congress. There were busy days of meetings, lectures and consultations, some lasting until well past midnight. I visited the Mauna Loa Observation Centre in the few free moments I had. The research station has undeniably shown that an increase in CO_2 concentrations in the atmosphere leads to global warming and has potentially very dangerous consequences. Data have been available for climate research since 1958. An analysis of these data permits us to better understand the present and the recent past and to make predictions for the future based on the knowledge of more than 60 years of research.

However, there is another source that provides climate data that easily predates Mauna Loa. Special drills are used to bore so deep below the surface of glaciers and ice sheets found in Greenland that they can reach the oldest ice layers. Cores of ice are extracted that contain trapped bubbles of atmospheric air, neatly sealed off from the outside world, the oldest studied being 800,000 years old. Scientists can detect evidence of atmospheric composition, volcanic eruptions and other factors from the ice bubbles. These data are combined with fossil and related records to reconstruct the profiles of past climates. These studies provide conclusive evidence that higher CO_2 concentrations in the atmosphere lead to higher temperatures and not vice versa. There is a linear relationship between the rise in temperatures and the rise in cumulative CO_2 concentrations. Until the Industrial Revolution, the concentration of CO_2 was around 300 ppm, but after that it skyrocketed. As frightening as these findings are, they also provide insight into the solution: if we can bring down greenhouse gas concentrations, temperatures will also fall. How do we apply what we have learned?

The public may not yet feel the effects of dangerously high atmospheric CO_2 levels. The pain will be felt by our children and grandchildren, and it will be irrevocable pain. The effects of atmospheric CO_2 manifest themselves after 30 to 40 years. In other words, the increase in the number and strength of hurricanes, heatwaves and floods that we observe today are the result of greenhouse gas emissions from 30 years ago. The amount of greenhouse gases in the atmosphere has increased by 47% in the past 50 years. Let this information sink in for a moment.

This means that even if we were to stop greenhouse emissions immediately, we must deal with the dangerous consequences of those emissions for the next 30 to 40 years. We must recognise that we do not know what effects this doubling of greenhouses gases will have, nor do we know if irreversible chain reactions already have been or will be triggered.

As frightening as findings are, they also provide insight into the solution: if we can bring down greenhouse gas concentrations, temperatures will also fall.

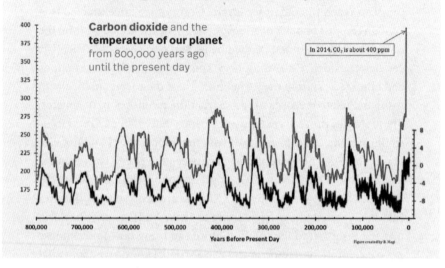

Global temperature strongly correlates with CO_2 levels over last 800,000 years

Carbon dioxide and the **temperature of our planet** from 800,000 years ago until the present day

In 2014, CO_2 is about 400 ppm

Years Before Present Day

Figure created by B. Magi

FIGURE: *The correlation of global temperature and CO2 levels*
SOURCE: IPCC – Intergovernmental Panel on Climate Change (2020)

Research from numerous institutes leads to the same conclusions about the relationship between CO2 and other greenhouse gases and the climate. Most of that scientific knowledge and evidence comes from the United Nations Intergovernmental Panel on Climate Change (IPCC). Its affiliated scientists examine the causes, consequences and risks of climate change and try to predict the realistic prospects. Since its establishment in 1988, the IPCC has issued regular reports. There has not been a single incidence of climate change being less severe than predicted in an earlier report.

Climate studies are ongoing at just about every university in the world in addition to the IPCC. This amassing of knowledge internationally and its exchange strengthens the scientific basis for climate problems and the proposal of solutions. This includes my region of Belgium and its neighbour the Netherlands; the results of collaborative and locally led research appears regularly in top scientific journals.

I enjoy following the research at Wageningen University (wUR) on the relationship of climate change to future food crops and production which, as I described earlier, can make a huge contribution to reducing greenhouse gases. In Belgium, I am involved in the Ecotron at Hasselt University, where I have been awarded an honorary doctorate degree. The Ecotron is a unique, high-tech research centre with equally high-tech ecosystem chambers, that can simulate the climate of the future. Hasselt University, together with other universities and international partners, uses the Ecotron to study the effects of climate change on our natural habitat and on agricultural crops. By all measures that lie within our means, internationally, the results are unequivocal: climate change is a fact, and it calls for swift action.

World leaders as climate protectors

The science is clear and shows irrefutably that we are facing major climate problems. Data from more recent developments since the start of the Industrial Revolution and data from how the climate has behaved over the past millions of years shows that we have entered a critical phase. Some of us may not have experienced it in our daily lives but it is there, nonetheless.

Climate change presents problems that we can afford to solve now. The longer we wait the more difficult and costly solutions will be. The nations of the world are already aware of the problem. The scientific evidence shows that a lack of action will lead to disastrous consequences. It is time for action by world leaders.

The first step towards managing climate change was the establishment in 1992 of the UN *Framework Convention on Climate Change (UNFCCC)* at the Earth Summit in Rio de Janeiro. It was agreed that member states that had ratified the UNFCCC would hold regular Conference of Parties (COP) meetings where they would discuss and create agreements to reduce greenhouse gas emissions. The next step major step was the UN *Kyoto Protocol (COP-3)* (1997), which assigned fixed time frames for meeting these agreed reductions. The protocol entered into force in 2005, and its first commitment period started in 2008 and ended in 2012. Meanwhile, more countries ratified the

UNFCCC under the pressure of accumulating and increasingly clear evidence that climate change has dangerous consequences for the planet and society.

As the first commitment period was in its final stages, a new agreement was in creation and was reviewed at the 2009 COP-15 negotiations in Copenhagen. Despite positive predictions, these negotiations failed, mainly because of disagreements between rich and poor countries over their reduction shares and reduction rates. A pressing new agreement was not yet possible, and world leaders bought extra time by extending the (old) Kyoto Protocol to 2020, a move known as the *Doha Amendment to the Kyoto Protocol* (2012). But even then, there was no time to waste, because getting a new agreement into force in 2020 takes time and a lot of negotiating.

Agreement was finally reached at the 2015 Paris Climate Summit (COP-21) to limit global warming to 1.5°C, 2°C maximum, to reduce greenhouse gas emissions as soon as possible and to achieve climate neutrality by 2050 at the latest. The *Paris Climate Agreement* was finally signed by 174 countries in New York on 'Earth Day' 22 April 2016.

The world cheered, but it would soon become clear that there is a big difference between signing an agreement and implementing the agreements made. A lot of governments struggled with internal conflict helped by convenient climate change doubters and fossil fuel industry lobbyists; CO_2 emissions continued to increase to their current levels which are 47% higher than they were to 50 years ago. Some governments tried to combat this phenomenon with attempts to speed up negotiations and expand the terms of the agreement.

The objective of the *Paris Climate Agreement* was simple: to reach zero emissions as soon as possible and no later than 2050. This would be done by calculating the Global Carbon Budget, which is the amount of CO_2 that can be emitted globally while staying below an increase of 1.5°C in global warming. This budget is a maximum of 400Gt CO_2. Annually, 40Gt CO_2 is emitted globally. Based on the Global Carbon Budget, a fair, solidarity-based (i.e., proportionally divided

Every tenth of a degree of extra warming that we can avoid would make a heaven-sent difference. Every tenth of a degree is worth fighting for. Action must be taken now.

between countries) and balanced burden-sharing estimate can then be made to determine the amount of CO_2 reduction each country has to achieve, wherein industrialised countries must make more efforts.

A simple calculation makes it clear that the global community has only 10 years left – and not until 2050 – to reach that target. This burden sharing is the basis of the *Paris Climate Agreement*: each member state takes responsibility to achieve its proportionate share of CO_2 reductions. Countries that do not comply obliges other member states to do more than agreed. An assessment of performance to date against targets reveals that many member states are not meeting the reduction targets they agreed to and that globally we are heading for a temperature rise of three degrees Celsius and more. This assessment has led to public protests. Greta Thunberg, the young Swedish activist, became world-famous through her personal protests that propelled her to a role as a figurehead of the global climate movement. Society slowly but surely is taking action on behalf of a liveable planet. Governments in numerous countries have been taken to court for failing to meet self-imposed targets and other governments have been accused of culpable omission and held liable for human rights violations and careless policies. These accusations have been upheld by judges in many countries.

Yet, again, with our future hanging by a thread, the agreement reached at the 2022 Sharm-el-Sheikh, Egypt Climate Summit in Egypt (COP 27) was disappointing. Yet, again, the ball was passed to the next climate summit in Dubai. Procrastination begat more procrastination. Believe me, there are several levels to hell. Every tenth of a degree of extra warming that we can avoid would make a heaven-sent difference. Every tenth of a degree is worth fighting for. Action must be taken now. There will be no partial wins in this game and no tied score. If we do not take action, we face a disaster. A disaster for every one of us.

When we talk about degrees of warming, we are referring to the increase in the earth's average temperature compared to pre-industrial times, before 1850, and before the use of fossil fuels skyrocketed during the Industrial Revolution. It's important to note that, because it's a global average, even small fractions of an increase in warming can have massive impacts. To reduce the devastation of a warming planet, we don't want to see any further rise in global average temperatures. Our world is already 1.15°C hotter than during pre-industrial times, and 1.5°C is the maximum level of warming we need to stay within if we are to avoid the worst impacts of the climate emergency.

A 1.5°C increase in temperature might sound fairly moderate, but it would still have a huge impact. This is particularly true for those living in poverty in the countries most vulnerable to the climate crisis. 1.5°C of warming will expose millions of people to more extreme climates, rising sea levels and more frequent weather-related disasters including heatwaves, drought, flooding and wildfires. We are already seeing these types of climate disasters make headlines every year, and any further rise in average temperature will only make their severity and frequency greater. What's more, these consequences of a warming world are hitting the world's poorest and most vulnerable communities hardest. Keep in mind that these countries have contributed the least to climate change. These temperature rises aren't just an environmental crisis, but a humanitarian one as well. In short, a world that's 1.5°C warmer is one that will need to adapt to all kinds of new struggles and injustices. We have a narrow window of opportunity to keep this as an achievable future and avoid the far worse scenarios which lie beyond that threshold.

So keep in mind: there are several levels to the hell we might face. Floodings, heatwaves, hurricanes or super rain cells, to name just a few, will be more prevalent, coming at us with more power and with devastating consequences for society. There will be a huge difference between 1.5°C and 1.6°C, or between 1.6°C and 2°C, and we cannot imagine just how disastrous a rise higher than 3°C will be. Once you realise this, you know that fighting for every milli-degree is worth it.

Citizens as climate protectors

When the leaders of our countries prove incapable of supporting the greater good, citizens have no choice but to take matters into their own hands. There are examples of this throughout history, including examples from the fight for our planet. Urgenda, the Dutch organisation for innovation and sustainability – led by fellow Goldman Environmental Prize winner Marjan Minnesma – together with 886 co-claimants, including myself, won a decision against the Dutch state on 24 June 2015. The court ruled that the Dutch government was obligated to reduce emissions urgently and significantly in line with its human rights obligations. The court ordered the Dutch state to reduce greenhouse gas emissions by 25% by 2020 compared to 1990 levels. The Dutch state appealed on grounds of causation, but this appeal was dismissed on 20 December 2019. This historic case was the first domino to fall, and it is regarded internationally as the most famous climate lawsuit to date.

What few had thought possible can happen after all. Urgenda and their lawyer Roger Cox made world news. With his book *Revolution Justified* (2015), the lawyer and ever-friendly nature lover gained international recognition for his stance that in cases of inadequate policy, climate targets can be enforced through the courts. *Milieudefensie Nederland*, a charity working on behalf of the environment, took oil giant Shell to court, and with the ruling on 26 May 2021 the world experienced another historic moment. The court ruled that the company must align its policies with the *Paris Climate Agreement* and that its net CO_2 emissions must drop by 45% by 2030 compared to 2019. This marks the first time ever that a company must align its policies with the *Paris Climate Agreement*.

These two legal cases bring hope for other groups of citizens who plan to take on powerful governments and companies on behalf of nature; to rethink what individuals can do to fight for our future, our very survival. Roger Cox was named one of the 100 most influential people on earth in 2021 by Time Magazine. Rightly so.

Currently, an estimated 2000 climate-related lawsuits have been launched worldwide in some 30 countries against governments and corporations. Society is stirring. Another domino fell in 2021 with the ruling of *L'Affaire du Siècle* (The Affair of the Century) in France. Several charities – *Notre Affaire à Tous, La Fondation pour la Nature et l'Homme*, Oxfam and Greenpeace – worked together to take the French government to court for inaction on climate issues and failure to meet its International, European and French obligations. The court ruled in favour of the claimants and ordered the government to reduce greenhouse gas emissions and to make reparations for the consequences of its inaction.

In Germany, a young farmer's wife was vindicated, supported by several fellow citizens and environmental organisations like Greenpeace. In her case, the German Constitutional Court ruled that the German federal Climate Act, which already targeted a 55% reduction in greenhouse gas emissions by 2030, violated the constitution for failing to sufficiently protect citizens, considering the growing evidence of climate change. Immediately, Angela Merkel's government acted, and less than a week later sharply increase its ambitions: the German reduction pathway will increase from 65% in 2030 to 88% in 2040 to net zero emissions in 2045. According to the latest in international climate science, these reductions are the bare minimum to avoid disaster scenarios.

What about my home country of Belgium? Together with some concerned friends I took the initiative to set up 'Warm Nest' in 2012, a discussion group that reflects on the biodiversity crisis and dangerous climate changes. We invited lawyer Roger Cox to join us in 2013 and it was a special evening. Four hours and a generous donation later, 11 'Concerned Flemings' decided – out of love for the planet – to set up the non-profit organisation KLIMAATZAAK and to progress a lawsuit where everyone wins. Here, too, the gauntlet was taken up by people like you and me. Eleven Concerned Flemings became 11,000 and eventually grew to more than 69,000 co-plaintiffs. The largest civil case ever in Belgium was initiated and citizens proved that their moral right should be defended and that the law was on their side. The court declared that the Belgian authorities were in default on 1 December 2014. It then took seven years of wrangling over language and procedures to reach a verdict. The Brussels court condemned the Belgian authorities for their negligent climate policies on 17 June 2021. The judges ruled that Belgian climate policy is so substandard that it violates the government's legal duty of care and human rights, just as the courts in the Netherlands and Germany had ruled. The court did not impose the requested reduction targets. An appeal was filed in early 2022 to provide for arguing that the reduction targets should be imposed.

Lastly, to make it clear that change isn't only possible in Europe, I would like to add one American example. In August 2023, in the first ruling of its kind in the US, a Montana state court ruled in favour of a group of young men and women who alleged that their state was violating their right to a 'clean and healthful environment' by promoting the use of fossil fuels. The court determined that a provision in the Montana Environmental Policy Act was effectively having a detrimental effect on the state's environment, and consequently on the young plaintiffs, because it prevented the state from considering the climate impacts of its energy projects. Eventually, the court ruled that the provision was unconstitutional, the court ruled. It was simply another decision of potentially monumental significance. Such a ruling might influence how judges handle similar cases in other states of the US.

How to move forward? The IPCC's latest assessment report – AR6 – makes no bones about it. Current measures to curb greenhouse gas emissions fall short of preventing large-scale climate disasters soon. Life on Earth as we know it will be irreversibly changed within a few decades. It is one of the strictest warnings ever given by the IPCC. That is because the IPCC dwells on so-called tipping points (chain reactions) in this report. When tipping points are reached, temperatures have passed such critical levels that there is an inevitable domino effect with disastrous consequences. Without immediate action, climate risks will accelerate and intensify, with dangerous impacts of climate change such as hurricanes, heat waves, and floods increasing not linearly but exponentially.

Note: once the 1.5°C warming limit has been passed, opportunities for and effectiveness of climate adaptation will shrink tremendously. At this point, I must give you an astonishing oversight of some relevant data. The average global temperature in 2022 was about 1.15 [1.02 to 1.27] °C above pre-industrial (1850-1900) levels. According to all datasets compiled by the World Meteorological Organization (WMO), 2022 was the 8th consecutive year (2015-2022) in which annual global temperatures have measured at least 1°C above pre-industrial levels.

2015 to 2022 have been the eight warmest years on record, fuelled by ever-rising greenhouse gas concentrations and heat accumulation, according to six leading international temperature datasets consolidated by the WMO. To conclude the rather unpleasant set of numbers: according to NASA, the first week of July 2023 was the hottest week ever recorded globally, with its global average temperature close to 17,24 °C on the 7th of July. This is 0.3°C above the previous record high of 16.94 °C, measured on 16 August 2016. Frightening.

It is dangerous to invest only in climate adaptation – currently a politically popular idea – because adaptation only alleviates the symptoms. It is not a structural solution! There is only one solution and that is to stop CO_2 emissions as soon as possible. Nature and climate do not have a pause button. We require acceleration, and not delay, to give ourselves and the younger generations a future.

A green revolution: acting beyond the boxes

As mentioned, biodiversity and climate are two sides of the same coin. What happens when climate change occurs and what is its impact on natural ecosystems and species of plants and animals?

I hope by now that I have convinced you that everything in the environment is interconnected with everything else and that you recognise that different species respond in different ways. With this in mind, the *Fifth Assessment Report* (WGII AR5, 2014) includes an overview of the shift that is occurring in the patterns of risks and of the potential benefits in response to climate changes for certain species. Many species live in very specific habitats and conditions and need the right climate to survive. In an increasingly warmer world, many species-specific conditions are changing relatively quickly. The speed of adaptation and the speed of movement of species towards a suitable habitat will determine the chances of survival for each species. Species try to move along with their – often shrinking suitable habitats – as it gets warmer. The speed can vary a lot between species. A tree moves much slower than a bird or a mammal. When the warming rate exceeds the species' movement speed, things often go wrong, simply because the conditions have become intolerable or because the habitats and ecosystems on which the species depends have disappeared. The following figure shows the maximum displacement rate of species groups per decade, not including birds. You can see that trees can relocate less than 20 km per decade so they are the least mobile and mammals that can relocate more than 100 km per decade are the most mobile.

You can flee from the heat to a new habitat if you are a bumblebee or bird, but if the new habitat does not have suitable trees, flowers and insects upon which you depend, you are likely to shrivel up and die. With the rapidly declining populations of species in mind, which the World Wildlife Fund mentions in the Living Planet Index, a lot of species will struggle. It is not just the flowers and the bees that will be victims of global warming, it will be us humans too, as our health and food supply will also come under increasing pressure.

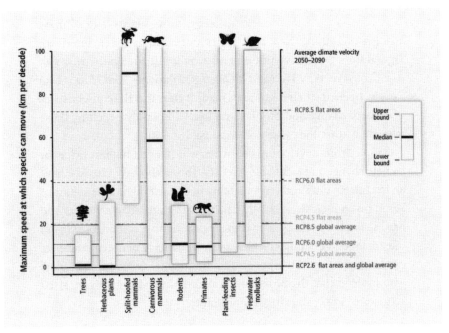

FIGURE: *The maximum rate at which species can move, juxtaposed against the rate at which temperature can change across landscapes*
SOURCE: IPCC Assessment Report 5 (2014)

COVID temporarily changed the world. But we have learned that – if we must – we can and should change very quickly. We will all have to look for a new normal, one where we must act inclusively. COVID has also taught us that pushing one button has consequences on other things, everything has to do with everything, just as in nature everything has to do with everything. Issues like climate change and biodiversity loss are both symptoms of a much larger systemic problem. By just trying to solve the climate problem, we shoot ourselves in the foot, because without a restoration of natural ecosystems, we are done for. You cannot save the world just by saving the climate.

Canadian publicist and activist Naomi Klein hit the nail on the head with the title of her 2014 book, *This Changes Everything: Capitalism vs. The Climate.* Her message was clear: 'Change now, before the climate changes everything'. New York Times journalist Thomas L. Friedman argued for a green revolution in his wonderful 2008 book *Hot, Flat and Crowded: Why We Need a Green Revolution – And How it Can Renew America.* Their arguments made it clear that the consequences of climate change and biodiversity loss will mainly be felt by those who are neither the cause nor responsible for it.

People from developing countries will pay the highest price for climate change and loss of biodiversity. Those who have caused it have an irrefutable duty and responsibility to devise and finance solutions based on an inclusive, socially balanced and sustainable vision. And here again, the message is that the transition to a sustainable system must happen very quickly. Inequality in damage between countries creates not only injustice but also environmental destruction. Leaders who pretend that the problem is too complicated to take concerted action are simply shirking responsibility.

> Leaders who pretend that the problem is too complicated to take concerted action are simply shirking responsibility.

Agriculture as the key agent of change

Pigeonholing agriculture

Agriculture has a key role in every point made in this chapter about biodiversity and climate. The topic of agriculture has become a politically loaded topic. Taking action is no longer a plaything of leftist and activist politicians, but a task for all of us, from left to right, progressive to conservative and conservationists to farmers.

What happens if we do not work together but toil away in our separate boxes instead? Here is one of many personal experiences of what not to do:

It was 2014. I was at the Brussels Square Congress Centre attending the Future of Agriculture Forum (FFA) as a panel member along with the European Commissioner for Nature Conservation, the Director of Agriculture and Environmental Services of the World Bank, the President of the German Landowners Association and the Chief Economist of the American Farm Bureau Federation.

The FFA is one of the most influential agriculture-oriented gatherings in the world and aims to have an open dialogue with the nature and environment sector. Sustainable food production and the Transatlantic Trade and Investment Partnership (TTIP – The Transatlantic Free Trade and Investment Treaty) were the central themes for the FFA. Pointed discussions about the treaty had been ongoing for some time. Proponents argued that the treaty would ensure economic growth, while opponents made the case that the agreement would further increase the power of big companies, making it difficult for governments to regulate agricultural practice.

The panel debate went well, I was able to keep my nerves under control, and after my plea for a transition to nature-inclusive agricultural practices, I was happy not to be asked any questions about the TTIP. The questions that did come my way I was able to answer. But a conversation from the night before reverberated in my mind.

I was one of a carefully selected group of about 30 people who were invited to dine in the private room of an upmarket restaurant in Brussels. Among those present were two EU commissioners, a dozen agriculture ministers from inside and outside Europe, secretaries-general and senior officials from Europe and the US, among others and some top lobbyists for crop protection and fertiliser products.

The theme of the evening was 'How to Feed the World' meaning how can food supplies be secured with a rising world population. 'These people could work together to make a difference if they wanted to', I thought to myself. I sat at the corner of the long table and paid close attention to the conversations going on around me. There seemed to be a double meaning in all that I heard. I suspected this was related to the impending Transatlantic Trade and Investment Partnership (TTIP).

Suddenly, one of the lobbyists spoke over all the others with a fervent plea for further industrialisation and demanding the alloca-tion of additional land for agricultural use. I gathered my courage, stood up and with my legs shaking I presented a counter-argument, saying that the lobbyist's demand was out of the question, that it would exacerbate the existing problems of loss of biodiversity. A few guests strained their necks to see who was talking, but the room was eerily silent. I quietly sat down and resumed my meal.

Later, during a heated discussion with one of the US lobbyists sitting next to me at the table, the lobbyist said: 'There is more than enough wasteland in the world, still plenty of space left for wildlife.' 'Dollars before life,' I thought, 'wasteland!' We must make do with the leftovers. I had the unpleasant feeling that practically the entire table thought the same way. The TTIP agreement was never ratified and the loss of wilderness lands to agriculture continues unabated.

A compartmentalised worldview with limited perspectives and the separation of functions leads to bad decisions. We have ample evi-dence of the consequences of this, of the adverse effects. The effect of our lifestyle on nature and climate are pertinent. We must deal with them. Can this provide an opening for inclusive thinking and the interweaving of functions?

About 190 million extra hectares of grassland and arable land have been taken up by agriculture in the last 50 years. This has taken a heavy toll on the proportion of wilderness on our planet. Wilderness accounted for 66% of the Earth's surface in 1937 dropping to about 35% in 2020. According to the report *Financing the Transition: The Costs of Avoiding Deforestation* (2023) from the Energy Transitions Commission, 10 football fields of forest disappear every minute somewhere in the world. As of 2018, we were losing 3.2 million hectares of primary forest every year, and this is without considering land lost to forest fires, which together represent a larger area than is being cut down every year.

Sustainable Development Goals (SDGs) targets were set in 2015 for 2030, and world leaders have agreed on measures in the various Conferences of Parties (COPs) to permit sustainable reversal. Each time, fine words are uttered, beautiful sentences are written, and ambitious new targets are agreed. This is all well and good, but we are behind schedule in many areas. We must find a way to accelerate the transition. Flowery speeches from yet another podium serve no purpose if we have not yet faced the facts of the damage caused by current agriculture practices.

A compartmentalised worldview with limited perspectives and the separation of functions leads to bad decisions.

Agricultural alarm bells

A recap of the facts. Every economic activity has an impact on the environment, including agriculture, and in particular the production of meat and poultry. Scientists are increasingly concerned about the environmental impact of meat consumption, as meat production – especially on an industrial scale as happens in many countries – contributes to biodiversity loss, soil erosion due to overgrazing, increasing consumption of carbon-containing fuels, increasing nitrogen and ammonia levels, excessive water use and increasing risks of viral diseases.

Far too large carbon footprint

One way to quantify the impact of agricultural practices is to calculate carbon footprints. According to the report *Greenhouse gas emissions from agrifood systems. Global, regional and country trends, 2000-2020,* by the United Nations Food and Agriculture Organization (FAO), agricultural and food systems cause one third of total anthropogenic (arising from mainly human activities) greenhouse gas emissions. In 2020, global emissions from agrifood systems reached 16 billion tonnes of carbon dioxide equivalent (Gt CO2eq), an increase of 9% since 2000. Emissions are generated by crop and livestock activities, by the dynamics of land use and by pre- and post-production processes, such as food production, retail, household consumption and food disposal.

According to the report *Tackling Climate Change through Livestock* (2013) by the United Nations Food and Agriculture Organisation (FAO), the global carbon footprint of meat production and livestock is 14.5% of all greenhouse gas emissions caused by human activities. Of this, 51% comes from beef cattle and 19% from dairy cattle. Pork and poultry – chickens and eggs – account for 9 and 8%, respectively. The rest comes from sheep, goats and buffalo.

According to Eurostat, the EU organisation that provides high-quality statistics and data, at the end of 2021, there were 142 million pigs, 76 million bovine animals and 71 million sheep and goats in the EU. The agricultural sector accounted for 11% of the EU's total domestic greenhouse gas emissions.

And what about those in my home country? Belgium's total livestock population was 58.2 million head in 2019, including 6.1 million pigs, 2.3 million cattle and 49.8 million poultry, accounting for 9% of total CO2 emissions. In Wallonia, the livestock population is rather small compared to Flanders. The total livestock population in Flanders is 52.7 million head in 2021, including 1.3 million cattle, 5.8 million pigs and 45.6 million poultry. In the Netherlands, the total livestock population is 116.5 million head in 2021, including 11.4 million pigs, 3.8 million cattle, 1.3 million goats and sheep and 99.9 million poultry. Total CO2 emissions from the agricultural sector are 16%, of which 68% come from livestock and manure processing.

Far too much nitrogen

Nitrogen (N2) is a colourless and odourless gas that is all around us. About 78% of all air consists of nitrogen. Nitrogen is one of the essential components that make up living matter, and so by itself is not harmful to humans and the environment.

Animal feed production accounts for 70% of the world's deforestation. Meat production requires much more water than vegetable production.

But there are also nitrogen-containing compounds emitted from our activities into the environment that can be harmful to humans and the environment. Nitrogen oxides (NOx) are mainly released when fossil fuels are burned, for example by road vehicles. There are also nitrogen compounds from farms, mostly in the form of ammonia (NH3). Farmers use manure from animals and artificial fertilisers to fertilise their land. Some of that manure evaporates as ammonia, polluting the air and being deposited into the soil and water. Excessive concentrations of nitrogen oxides and ammonia have a very detrimental effect on nature and threaten biodiversity.

Global livestock concerns have significantly altered nitrogen fluxes in recent years, threatening the environment and human health. A report published in Nature, *Nitrogen emissions along global livestock supply chains* (2020), calculates the impact of livestock production on global nitrogen flows and emissions. The livestock industry's emissions are about 65 teragrams (Tg) of nitrogen per year. This means that nitrogen emissions for meat and dairy production alone exceed the lower limit of the 62 to 82 Tg per year that is considered the 'planetary limit'.

Said otherwise: the safe global level for nitrogen emissions is already at levels that put humanity's future at risk. The results show that the livestock industry currently represents one third of current man-made nitrogen emissions and that the amount of nitrogen pollution emitted by the global livestock industry is greater than the planet can handle. 68% is related to livestock feed production. Most emissions come from locally produced food of animal origin, although nitrogen emissions in international trade, arising from industry and transport, are significant for some countries.

The Netherlands and my region of Flanders in Belgium play a sad leading role internationally. A portion of protected nature areas suffer from far too high nitrogen concentrations. This should not be surprising. The bigger the livestock, the bigger the problem.

Far too much water needed

Besides taking up extra space for agriculture and the climatic impact of livestock waste and grazing, meat production requires a lot of water, especially for growing animal feed. Animal feed production accounts for 70% of the world's deforestation. Thus, meat production requires much more water than vegetable production. The Institution of Mechanical Engineers states that producing 1 kilogram of meat requires between 5,000 and 20,000 litres of water, while producing 1 kilogram of wheat requires between 500 and 4,000 litres of water and 1 kilogram of potatoes requires only 287 litres of water. Compared to meat production, vegetable foods therefore require significantly less water.

Far too many farm animals

Another eye-opener. In a report entitled *Distribution of Biomass on Earth*, published in 2018 in the *Proceedings of the National Academy of Sciences*, the authors showed that 82% of all biomass on Earth is found in plants which seems plausible. They reported that the 7.8 billion people on the planet represent only 0.01% of this, which is much more surprising. Here is the explanation: Farm mammals like cows and pigs make up 60% of mammalian biomass, humans make up 36% and wild mammals the remaining 4%, a staggeringly small portion of the whole. And calculating the biomass of birds shows a similar picture. Poultry makes up 70% of the biomass of all birds with only 30% being wild birds. It puts the proportions in biomass terms in perspective: only 4% for wild mammals and only 30% for wild birds. The number of chickens worldwide has more than doubled since 1990. In 2019, there were some 25.9 billion chickens, up from 14.38 billion in 2000. And what does that say about us? Our 0.01% is trivial but our impact, on the other hand…?

Far too much meat consumption

We consumers love meat. Many people just cannot resist it, even though they know that with every chew they are working against the climate. But it is so tasty and that's why we chew on and on. According to the United Nations Food and Agriculture Organization (FAO), between 1990 and 2009, total global meat consumption increased by almost 60% and per capita consumption by almost 25%. Meat consumption is expected to continue increasing by 1.7% a year until 2022. Argentines currently eat the most beef, at almost 40 kilograms per person per year. Residents of the 27 countries of the European Union and China eat the most pork, about 35.5 and 30.4 kilograms per capita per year respectively. Israelis, in turn, eat the most poultry, with 64.9 kilograms per person per year. Residents of Kazakhstan eat the most sheep, at 8.5 kilograms per person per year.

If the negative impact of meat eating is so great and damaging for the planet and, in turn, for society, what should we eat in say 2050? Will we be able to adapt our eating habits by then? According to the report by the EAT-Lancet Commission, global consumption of fruit, vegetables, nuts and pulses will have to double, and consumption of foods like red meat and sugar should be reduced by more than 50%. Eat more fruit and vegetables, more whole grains, less junk food and less meat and dairy. If we can move our eating habits in this direction, we increase the chances of reducing the incidence and severity of some diet-related diseases and of bringing down the carbon and biodiversity impacts of our diet.

But things do not seem to be moving in the right direction. For large parts of the world, eating meat is a luxury they are reluctant to give up, just as we in the West saw eating meat as a sign of progress after World War II. Quite a few regions have a distinct culture involving excessive meat consumption and other cultures seem keen to adopt this behaviour as an expression of prosperity, yet it is not appropriate to extend this trend to the rest of the world. It would simply make our planet uninhabitable. The impact of industrial farming is so disruptive and destructive that this form is no longer defensible.

In his recent book *Regenesis* (2022), George Monbiot, British activist, writer and journalist with *The Guardian* newspaper, UK, believes that our food system is inadequate and will crash. According to Monbiot, the 75 billion animals we currently raise in barns and other enclosures cause more climate damage than all planes, cars, trucks and ships combined. He believes that the agricultural system must be shaken up and we will have to evolve to a totally new system with steaks from breweries to algae farming to the magic of bacteria in the soil. The difficulty is our identity is deeply rooted and co-determined by the food we consume. But with the right approach, we have the means to save the planet.

But what about all those farmers who now earn their living in agriculture and who have gone to great lengths to constantly adapt to new local, national and international regulations? Farmers who often had no choice but to join the rat race and often had to go deeply into debt to implement new regulations. Is there a future for agriculture? Yes indeed, for the simple reason that we humans will not get very far without food and drink. Farming is not under threat.

The question is not whether there is still a future, but rather which future will we choose. It seems reasonable that we should say goodbye to a few excesses in agriculture. Having chickens that are endlessly bred to produce as much meat as possible in just six weeks should no longer be one of them. In the future, we will be surprised that we ever bred animals this way. There will also have to be reasonable alternatives to the industrial meat industry and to salmon full of antibiotics. The reduction of livestock is written in the stars because the gains for nature, climate, farmers and society are too great. It is no longer justifiable to raise millions of pigs or cows or chickens – often in conditions where the animals suffer or live in unhealthy conditions and are prone to viral and other diseases that could be passed to other animals and humans. The transition away from industrial meat practices will have to be quick and it will not be painless. But I sincerely hope the industry embraces this transition as a sustainable opportunity. We can all lend a helping hand. It is us, the consumers who elect our politicians, along with the government who should take responsibility in providing a reasonable alternative for the agricultural industry.

The essential transitions needed in agriculture must not fall on the shoulders of individual farmers. There are enough locals in every region who know where we need to go, but there is also enough lobbying going on to stymie the needed reforms. European agricultural policy, for example, still seems stuck in policies of the past. The policies protect the interests of parties that influenced the content of these policies. But there is an opportunity to do things differently in a fair and responsible way. The agriculture sector must be given the chance to enable a sustainable transition.

There is an opportunity to do things differently in a fair and responsible way. The agriculture sector must be given the chance to enable a sustainable transition.

For now, however, some entrenched structures will need to be relaxed. The European Agricultural Policy (CAP – Common Agricultural Policy) is rightly contested because the results so far are rather meagre for sustainability and greening. Considering that 50% of the European Union's total budget goes to agriculture, you might expect more. Under the CAP, the EU-subsidised expansion of scale simply continues, even as the negative impacts on nature and climate are frighteningly clear. The funding mechanism that provides income and product support favoured large and especially convenient agricultural structures. So, whether the new European agricultural policy from farm to fork as part of the EU Green Deal will initiate the turnaround to sustainability remains to be seen.

We, as consumers and members of the voting public and our food suppliers, have responsibilities alongside national and European politicians. The agriculture of the future will have to transform itself into sustainable bio-agriculture producers and from meat-oriented to plant-based businesses. We must adapt our western eating habits, which will not be easy. The transformation has already begun, including at the level of multinational. Unilever acquired the Vegetarian Butcher and there have been many investments in meat alternatives coming from bioindustry. There are significant developments in the field of cultured meat products. Meat replacement vegan products are also on the rise and are almost ready to break through globally. 'We don't need a handful of vegans eating plant-based food perfectly,

> The impact of tens of millions of people who eat vegetarian or vegan occasionally or regularly is greater than that of a small (but growing) group that is fully committed to it.

we need millions of people doing it imperfectly', as I recently read somewhere on Facebook. The impact of tens of millions of people eating vegetarian or vegan occasionally or regularly is obviously greater than that of a small (but growing) group that is fully committed to it. If you are interested in veganism, be sure to read the fantastic book, *How to Create a Vegan World*, by friend and fellow Ashoka Fellow, Tobias Leenaert (Ashoka Fellows are a group of social innovators). The description of the road to Veganville is a wonderfully lucid description by this deep thinker and 'slow-opinionist'. You can start on the road to a Vegan diet today. Every little bit helps.

Politicians, citizens and industry must lead by example, allowing and encouraging agriculture to move with them. For instance, a sustainable agricultural transition will have to be accompanied by an assured higher income for farmers. In my experience, many farmers are willing to transition and are looking for a way to do it. We need to offer them support when they reach out and cherish their actions.

An interesting development is taking place almost silently in the countryside. Farmers and conservationists are moving away from the idea that they are natural enemies and finding that there is much more to be gained through cooperation than to be tangled in a web of opposition. As president of EUROPARC Federation, the largest network of protected natural areas in Europe, I have visited natural regions in more than 30 European countries over the past seven years. What I have seen is farmers proudly selling their products in national park visitor centres and the formation of new alliances between farmers and conservationists. Everyone is learning from everyone else, for example, that land-based agriculture is largely dependent on soil fertility and soil biodiversity: the more soil biodiversity, the better; that biological control – such as using parasitic wasps instead of insecticides – is often more effective in controlling pests; that the proximity of natural elements in the immediate neighbourhood acts as a buffer against soil erosion and has a positive effect on farm management and product quality. Conversely, we know that these natural elements – such as hedges, hedgerows, ditches and ponds – perform important functions for the survival and exchange of species and habitats. Somewhere along the way, we forgot that the separation of activities has far more disadvantages than advantages.

Ashoka, Everyone a Changemaker

We need to learn from each other to move forward together. Everyone is welcome. Albert Einstein was convinced that everyone can be a genius, but suppose you judge a fish only on its ability to climb a tree, that fish will spend its entire life thinking it cannot do anything. Sustainable business, or sensible farming, is a process of constant learning and trying. That is what we try to do in the Bioregional Weaving Labs Collective, an initiative of Ashoka Netherlands in which I am on the design team and closely involved. The Bioregional Weaving Labs Collective is a growing group of more than 25 international system-changing organisations and socio-ecological entrepreneurs seeking to restore landscapes through collective action with farmers, conservationists, communities and stakeholders. Using internationally successful models, we aim to restore, regenerate and protect one million hectares of terrestrial and marine landscapes in Europe over the next decade. Ten Bioregional Weaving Labs will demonstrate 'hands on' that a sustainable transition is possible. During the same period, we will engage local communities and aim to support one million people who want to help achieve their dreams.

Ashoka is the world's largest social organisation of entrepreneurs pursuing sustainable systemic change from hybrid thinking and doing, often embedded in society. 'Everyone a changemaker' is Ashoka's motto, meaning that everyone can do something that can lead to change.

A pact for open space

We must solve biodiversity and climate challenges together. Parties who are often in hostile opposing camps must learn to collaborate; to unite their knowledge and experience and find solutions together. Too often the media exacerbates differences between parties who wish to use open land and those who wish to protect it. Imagine if both sides were to make a 'pact for open space' and build a broad coalition to designate land under dispute as standstill territory. With the current possibilities of it and data processing at hand, accounting could easily be established at the municipal, provincial and national levels, and negotiations for the use of land could be carried out between them. The principle would be that if something were added to the countryside, we would need to demolish an existing structure or release other land in compensation. This concept would need to be implemented carefully and thoughtfully, with the priority being that new space-consuming structures replace old infrastructure and do not encroach on open space.

I argue alongside a pact for open space, under the banner of 'vat inclusive'. There are examples of farmers and conservationists building strong coalitions based on a foundation of trust and led by camaraderie rather than being undermined by opposition and suspicion. If we dare to look closely, we can see the unfolding of a sustainable agricultural transition that we hope can soon become systemic. A pact for open space, 'vat inclusive'. This means quality protection, restoration and design of open space with 'Proof of Added Value'. It means producing high-quality food in an interwoven nature-rich landscape that can act as a corridor for plants and animals and guarantee a sustainable income for farmers. These are developments I have seen all around me among farmers and conservationists, a process in which there are only winners. Regional products are a good example, because of the multiple benefits they provide. Combining farming with a more natural infrastructure – like hedges, ponds or small forests – increases pollination, stores more CO_2, prevents the disappearance of local food cultures and traditions and combats people's dwindling interest in the food they eat, in where it comes from and how our food choices affect the world around us.

The answers of organic farming

The FAO report *The World of Organic Agriculture 2021* summarises the statistics and emerging trends of organic agriculture. By 2021,

72.3 million hectares of farmland in 187 countries will be organically managed by at least 3.1 million farmers. Global sales of organic food and drink exceeded 106 billion euros in 2019. Meanwhile, while too much remains the same in Europe in agriculture, there is also a quiet organic farming revolution taking place. It is a hopeful story, but it is one that needs additional attention.

Let us focus on European plans on the matter, for example. One target the European Union has set is to have 25% of its agricultural area designated as organic farming by 2030. This share of organic farming is already increasing, rising from 5.8% in 2012 to 9.1% in 2020. This would in itself be encouraging news, were it not that the rate of converting land would need to be four times higher than this to reach the 25% target by 2030. What is encouraging, is that the impact of organic agriculture on nature and society can no longer be denied. Spain has the largest area devoted to organic farming in Europe, followed by France and Italy. Agro-ecological projects, often through new cooperatives, are springing up like mushrooms. A current shorter-term objective is to reach 15% of land designated for organic farming by 2031, and extra support under the European Green Deal and the new Common Agricultural Policy (CAP) could accelerate progress. However, reaching the target will still be challenging.

The preservation and restoration of biodiversity are included in the EU's CAP objectives. As consumers, we can help produce food closer to home, either by literally getting involved or by becoming clients of local producers. The concept of a shorter chain from farm to our homes is gaining ground. Growing food close to home seems wonderfully innovative, but it is a step forward to a common practice of the past where the surrounding countryside brought the food to the village or city via a short chain. However, this sustainable agricultural transition should not become a privilege for those who can afford it, but one that is affordable for all. The search for models that are also socially balanced may safely receive much more attention, but again, interweaving and exchanging ideas, strategies, projects and involving as many interest groups as possible would be of benefit.

In this chapter, I have addressed biodiversity, climate change, our role as consumers and the role of industry and agriculture. I have used figures and personal experiences to show how, in nature, everything is connected to everything else and that we must learn from this when designing our economy and agriculture. This can be done by large farmers, but also by small agricultural entrepreneurs, in which we consumers can play an important role. I have shown that, globally, we are destroying the climate at breakneck speed and why grassroots campaigns and citizen-led legal challenges on their own will not be enough. We need an integrated approach. We need committed leadership.

The answer is at hand for our planet, for industry, for agriculture and for us as consumers and citizens. It starts with daring to think outside the box. If we work with nature, nature will push us further and work with us.

Continue reading and you will learn that farmers turn out to be very good at doing business with nature conservationists. The government can support both the market and nature by creating attractive financial conditions. Individuals like you and me can be surprisingly good at getting others to move. Continue reading to learn about my (Re) connection Model. This is a model for cooperation between scientists and residents and between biologists and entrepreneurs, in an impressive nature park where economy and ecology are not opponents, but loyal and valuable partners. A place where everyone loves to be and where those who formerly minded the land have built new, lucrative and sustainable lives. The (Re)connection Model shows that earning money and caring for nature are complementary, in a model where citizens, entrepreneurs and governments dare to walk off the beaten track. Turn the page, and I will explain it to you....

Chapter 3

"Gutta cavat lapidem, non vi,
sed saepe cadendo.
*The drop hollows out the stone,
not by violence,
but by falling often.*"

– Choerilus of Samos (second half of 5th century BC)

TOWARDS A DIFFERENT ECONOMIC MODEL

The (Re)connection Model: inspiration
for a pact between ecology and economics

We have come to regard nature, in the last centuries, as the source of our food and a place where we can entertain ourselves after work, a luxury that exists for our pleasure. We have made half-hearted efforts here and there to protect nature, but we have seen this mostly as a cost burden. We have learned to build a tourism industry, carefully separating the hedonistic exploitation of nature from the frenetic protection of the scraps left over after the tourist has done his thing. We have never learned how to truly value nature, to recognise its astronomical value, a value that even the most sophisticated models cannot quantify. We can assign economic values to all other types of human activity, but no number has ever been assigned to nature. Strange.

But new ideas on how to arrive at a more nature-inclusive economy are emerging. The (Re)connection Model, which I developed and rolled out with support from a group of very clever people, is based on the idea of creating a nature-inclusive economy. It is a reversal in thinking where nature is seen not as a barrier, not as a cost, but as the most important part of the solution. The model provides a means to benefit both people and nature and build a healthy planet. It is simply attributing a fair and just value to nature. In this chapter, I explain how the model works.

The value of nature

We assign value to things in an arbitrary way. Take the tree frog that I described in the introduction, the one that looked at me with its big eyes and made me realise that we should invest in nature. Would you be able to tell me how much that tree frog is worth? Or Paris's Notre-Dame cathedral, what would be its value? Is it determined only by the cost of the materials it was built from? Or what value would we give to a banknote if we don't read the numbers on it? Its intrinsic value is practically zero, it is valued by *what it represents to us humans*. The value of a forest, a church, a banknote or a tree frog is determined by the value we attribute to it.

It is not difficult to explain that nature is, in fact, invaluable. Nature gives us life and health; it is the basis of most of our medicines. When we inhale, we inhale nature, it integrates with us, fuels our bodies and envelops us. Through nature we experience beauty and feel part of something bigger than ourselves. Yet we treat nature as if it has no value and is something to be used and discarded and then we resent the costs of discarding it. So we can assign value to disposing of nature, but we cannot assign a value to nature itself. This is a world turned upside down.

Dutch poet Lucebert wrote, 'Everything of value is defenceless.' He was right. The value of nature is so infinite that it cannot be put into figures. However, we must do our best to try and assign that value nonetheless, to try and calculate the incalculable. Nature's beauty alone, its 'wildness' and our dependence on it for our very lives should give it an intrinsic value and make it an obvious thing to protect. Alas, the intrinsic value of nature does not outweigh our desire to exploit it for financial gain. A common misconception is that nature only adds to the cost base. Let me sum up how wrong this thinking is.

At least 40% of the global economy and 80% of the needs of poor populations depend on natural ecosystems. But are the bees, the moors, the marshes, the coral reefs and the Amazon Forest paid enough for their contribution, for their diligent work? On the contrary, they get nothing in return. I am not alone in trying to calculate the economic value of nature. I refer you to the *European Biodiversity Strategy 2030*. The authors estimated that more than half of global gross domestic product (GDP)[2] depends on the services provided to us by natural ecosystems. Despite this, our current economic thinking is that we have a right to accept nature's contribution free of charge.

According to the World Economic Forum's *Global Risks Report 2023*, climate change and biodiversity loss are the biggest risks to the global economy over the next decade. So we can no longer really afford to see nature as something that has no value. According to a recent report by the United Nations Food and Agriculture Organization (FAO), biodiversity loss threatens food security. A loss in biodiversity would force us to depend on an ever-decreasing number of species to feed ourselves. In short, we depend entirely on nature for the air we breathe, the water we drink, the materials we use, for a stable climate, for our food and for our health, inspiration and happiness.

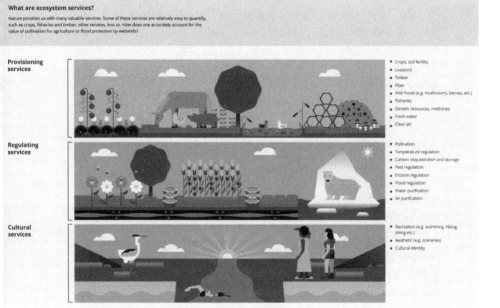

FIGURE: *Mapping ecosystem services*

SOURCE: European Environment Agency – Infographic

2 I use the long scale definition of the word 'trillion' of 10 to the 18th power, not the common short scale meaning of the word as one million million or 10 to the 12th power.

Nature is worth much more than we realise in everyday life. In fact, that value is so great that the 'nature bank' certainly offers the greatest guarantees of survival and is consequently the best bank in the world. Investing in nature therefore is investing in ourselves.

Our planet and our societies would look very different if we would invest on behalf of nature, if we would begin to reimburse nature for all that nature has contributed on our behalf. It is time for recovery, time for nature to recover the space and value it deserves. Benjamin Franklin, a founding father of the US, said, 'If you fail to prepare, you prepare to fail.' If we need to finance change, we need to change finance. The more evidence we can provide of the existential value of nature, the more people will connect, and the more value nature will have. It is high time to act accordingly.

We only need to calculate the so-called 'ecosystem services' to work out what nature is worth, i.e., the socio-economic value and health value of natural ecosystems. So, what exactly are we talking about when we talk about ecosystem services? In simple terms, they are the services that nature provides to humans, often for free. There are different types of ecosystem services:

1   *Producing ecosystem services* provide material products, such as food, drinking water and wood.
2   *Regulating ecosystem services* include processes such as water purification, climate regulation and pollination.
3   *Cultural ecosystem services* include the opportunities ecosystems provide us such as recreation, relaxation, cognitive development, inspiration and spirituality.

Ecosystem services can be used to support arguments about the value added by nature. The concept of ecosystem services helps us to realise that nature adds value and does not belong on the cost side of value equations. Nature is maybe the most important and highest value asset of all.

We must remember that the marine ecosystem also has an incalculable intrinsic value and that the economic value of the marine ecosystem is mind boggling. According to a report by the World Wildlife Fund, the marine ecosystem is valued at USD 24 trillion. It is a staggering amount: the number 24 followed by 18 zeros.[3] The marine ecosystem produces half the oxygen we breathe and stores 30% of the greenhouse gases that we produce. In other words, the oceans act as underwater forests and temper our planet's rising thermostat.

Do you know the value of a view of the ocean? Simple answer: buy a house in the Los Angeles region with a sea view. Ask yourself how many tourists are attracted by the sea and how many ate attracted by an industrial region. A view of nature or a view of the sea are prerequisites for the huge economic added value generated. The economic (added) value results from the intrinsic quality and not the other way around. Provided you are smart about it. If one is not careful things can go completely wrong.

The tourism industry reappraised

The value of nature on land and in the sea is astronomical when calculated in ecosystem services. The value of nature in economic terms is demonstrated repeatedly by the tourism industry; an observation that is considered taboo in the world of nature conservation. This is probably justified because tourism companies do not include ecosystem services in their profit and loss calculations. The value of nature is not recognised, leading to the exploitation of nature.

The tourism industry income is not only derived from city trips but also, increasingly, from travel destinations where visitors can enjoy the beauty of nature. The tourism industry is a major contributor to the global economy. According to the World Travel & Tourism Council, tourism represented 10.4% of global gross domestic product (2019) and it provided 334 million jobs – that is one in 10 jobs worldwide. Tourism is the main source of income for many developing countries. On the other hand, tourism has a huge negative ecological footprint and is the fourth largest source of pollution. The share of nature-based

---

3 Gross domestic product (GDP) is the total value of all goods and services produced within a country's borders. It is the main measure of a country's market value. Increases and decreases in GDP are a measure of the development of the economy.

tourist destinations is estimated at 20%. Revenue from the tourism industry and the damage it does to nature are calculated independently, in separate silos. What I mean by that is that calculations are often handled in a separate way that does not include ecosystem services in the profit-and-loss forecasts. Working in silos in this way ignores the (negative) impact of tourism as well as it prevents any acknowledgment of the opportunities in which an appreciation (and protection) of nature and attention to revenues can coexist, or even thrive. By calculating in silos, costs and benefits are misinterpreted, with huge threats both for nature and for tourism as a result.

What we need to do is think differently, think more logically about the value of the tourism industry. Let me try to explain. Tourism often involves a spatial aspect. City trips in New York, Barcelona or Paris are popular, but sometimes the space itself is the destination. Think, for instance, of a beautiful, undeveloped coastal region, an unspoilt landscape, a national park or a Unesco Biosphere Reserve. You can think of this area-based tourism as a unique sub-segment of the tourism industry, because not all tourist attractions are spatial entities. Visiting Barcelona is of course also about space, but what if the attraction is open, naked space or is a pristine natural landscape? This can lead to tensions if you want to build on the open space, erecting bungalow parks or hotels which occupy the space that was the reason to come. A hotel near Barcelona's Sagrada Família may not affect the beauty of the magnificent cathedral, but a hotel in a national park can destroy the essence of the park itself. It is good to remember that tourism is always a consequence of a certain quality, and not the other way around. If the quality of the environment or services is degraded and disappears, tourism will also disappear.

Tourism is always the consequence of a certain quality, and not the other way around. If that quality disappears, tourism will also disappear.

There is often something destructive in the DNA of traditional tourism. You start with the view of the sea or a mountain range, or in the case of a national park, for example, beautiful vistas and marshes. That quality attracts people, and the needs of the visitor need to be served. There is nothing wrong with that. But often the distinctive quality of the destination suffers or is lost in meeting the needs of visitors. Time and again, the beautiful coastal and dune areas have been ruined by unrestrained and ill-considered tourist-economic developments. As soon as the distinctive quality is spoiled, tourists move on to the next coast or subtropical island.

> Disrespectful exploitation and mass tourism degraded the tropical island of Haad Rin into one big ecological disaster and huge dump in a decade: nature gone, tourism gone, population bankrupt.

There are countless examples of this. The breathtakingly beautiful tropical Haad Rin, in southern Thailand, was 'discovered' by tourists in the 1970s. Soon after, this natural gem was inexpertly developed as a top tourist destination by a few tourism entrepreneurs. After all, nature was taken for granted, it was thought of as ever-present. You have undoubtedly guessed the result: for a short period, Haad Rin was a tourist paradise on earth and a licence to print money for a few entrepreneurs. But disrespectful exploitation and mass tourism relegated the place to one big ecological disaster and a huge dump within a decade: nature gone, tourism gone, population bankrupt. And who paid nature back what was taken from it?

Tourism can be either a curse or a blessing. It is my belief that we must chose now to make tourism of the future sustainable. Tourism's ecological footprint today is an important touchstone for tomorrow's tourism. Sustainable tourism considers the carrying capacity of both nature and the local population. To ensure sustainability, co-investments must be made in the protection of nature because it is understood that natural heritage provides the distinctive quality and is a prerequisite for success.

We must somehow compensate nature for the value extracted from it and include it in calculations. Fair is fair. Within area-based tourism, where space per se (nature) is the destination, sea views or the presence of extensive, high-quality nature contribute to the value of a destination and its financial returns. It is important to be aware of the value of nature when, for example, seeking funding to maintain beaches and dunes. The necessary investments in nature are too often seen as costs only. But the costs are investments in maintaining and improving the asset (nature) to increase the magnitude

Within area-based tourism, where nature is the destination, sea views or the presence of extensive, high-quality nature contribute to the value of a destination and its financial returns.

of returns from the tourist destination. The income easily compensates for the investments made. Think of the income generated directly and indirectly by governments such as overnight surcharges, VAT recovery, additional income through taxes, and so on. Or think of the extra revenue for a hotel owner with an organic garden or vegetarian menu, all tailored to the carrying capacity and quality of the region.

If one considers the overall costs for maintaining nature, when it is the central reason for attracting tourists versus returns, the income easily compensates for the investments made. By rethinking how we view the 'natural capital' of a business, we create an opportunity for ourselves and for nature. The (Re)connection Model offers proof that sustainable area-based tourism can be an incentive to improve the intrinsic quality of a space and that the investment costs are minimal compared to the returns.

New: bringing nature into the equation

Under the colonial system, we equated the costs of labour of slaves with the cost of food and shelter. We had somehow convinced ourselves, had deluded ourselves into thinking, that this was a fair exchange. Radical thinking was required to change this practice and begin paying a proper wage. The same applies to nature. We are all exploiting it. We need to rethink our calculations for the debt we owe to nature for its contributions.

As explained earlier in this book, a purely growth-based economy is fatal to the viability of our planet and society. The current dominant economic system needs constant expansion to avoid collapsing. But continued reliance on this model will continue to drive climate change and culminate inevitably in ecological collapse. The dominant economic system is simply destructive to people and to the planet.

Is there an alternative? Companies measure growth based on profits; a country's economic growth is measured by calculating its gross domestic product (GDP). The calculation of GDP is a one-sided economic materialist approach that does not reflect the depletion and destruction of the ecosystems on which the economy is built nor the wellbeing of people and society. European society is based on a rich tradition of values that eclipse mere materialistic consumption, like human dignity, freedom, democracy, equality, health and appreciation of the diversity of our natural heritage. Surely the growth of society cannot be reduced to a mere economic metric like GDP.

Western economic thinking goes back a few centuries. Four hundred years ago, the Dutch United East India Company (VOC) operated under the premise that nature and human life could be destroyed at will to satisfy the desires of shareholders. *The Nutmeg's Curse*, written by Indian author Amitav Ghosh, describes how the Dutch VOC mentality of those days still drives the world today and that it is this mentality that has plunged us into the climate change and biodiversity crisis.

It is now time to define 'growth' differently. Measurement of growth should encompass the wellbeing of people and the environment. We need to develop new methodologies for measuring growth that incorporate vital ecosystems, sustainability and fundamental values. We need to create innovative and socially balanced lifestyles, enthuse communities to participate and develop conditions that are attractive for everyone. This is only possible if we stop exceeding the environmental capacity of our planet, as illustrated in Johan Rockström's figure in the first chapter.

Our focus on perpetual growth and our enabling of a disposable economy to drive perpetual growth must be replaced by a new economic model. Many new ideas on how to shape our economic reality in the future are emerging. Innovative thinkers, such as Mariana Mazzucato, are developing new economic models that highlight the leading role of governments. Or Kate Raworth who has devised the promising doughnut economy, in which the economy is defined by planetary and social boundaries, and thus stays within the carrying capacity of the earth. Both are working with world leaders to find new ways to incorporate nature into economic models.

An increasing group is supporting 'Degrowth', a movement that argues that social and ecological harm is caused by the pursuit of infinite growth

A reversal in our attitudes and actions can be rapid by adjusting or replacing our attention to the GDP, which to date in no way reflects the value of natural capital, our wellbeing and sense of happiness. and western development imperatives. Others support – and yet again others also oppose – the decoupling of economics and ecology, whereby the economy would be allowed to grow without a corresponding increase in additional environmental and natural constraints. In turn, The Economics of Ecosystems and Biodiversity (TEEB) is an internationally accepted and successful methodology for calculating 'natural capital', the value of the services provided to us by nature. TEEB is an international initiative to draw attention to the global economic benefits of biodiversity. It aims to highlight the growing costs of biodiversity loss and ecosystem degradation and bring together expertise from the natural sciences, economics and policy to enable practical action. This initiative is being taken seriously.

We have developed a new understanding about inclusiveness and interconnectedness and that nature is an inseparable part of the economic process. A one-sided society organised solely to promote growth sets off alarm bells because it leads irrevocably to the destruction of nature and of ourselves. The cry for help – a planetary sos – has never sounded louder: 'Save the planet to save ourselves!'

It is urgent that we reverse our thinking because we can only save ourselves by saving the planet. Or in other words, if we save the tree frog, then the tree frog will save us. Perhaps the solution is contained in the problem, where the barriers and obstacles can be removed from within to achieve a sustainable and nature inclusive transition faster and more efficiently.

Do we face an impossible task? The reversal can be rapid if we adjust GDP or replace it by a better measure of the value of natural capital, our wellbeing, and our state of contentment. The UN has recently adopted a new measurement tool that could be a game changer. The System of Environmental Economic Accounting (SEEA), or Ecosystem Accounting for short, is a new international framework that takes natural capital into account when measuring economic prosperity as well as peoples' wellbeing. Less industrialised and urbanised countries, i.e. many developing countries, are higher ranked by SEEA than by GDP. This could make them eligible for more opportunities related to the restoration of wildlife, for example, or to combat global warming. The poverty of the past will then become the wealth of the future.

Including nature in national budgets is a trend that is being emulated worldwide. By 2021, more than 90 countries established SEEA accounts and many more are planning to establish such accounts. Including biodiversity and natural ecosystems as assets on the balance sheet of GDP, valuing them economically and evaluating them annually – increase or decrease in nature assets – is an important 'ancillary' argument to prove the 'inestimable' intrinsic value of nature and make it clear to policymakers that economics without ecology is impossible. In the same vein, the (Re)-connection Model was inspired by SEEA. The model entails a reversal in thinking. We did not regard nature as a barrier, or as a cost item, but as the most important part of a solution to the state we are in.

The (Re)connection Model explained

Economy and ecology

The Model is an excellent example of how by turning thinking around, nature can be seen as an asset instead of a cost. It is a practical example for demonstrating that ecology and economy need not be seen as two separate entities, but as an integrated whole. The Model shows that saving nature means saving ourselves, and that saving nature helps to create a situation where people in the neighbourhood can also earn a good living. It shows too that if you give nature a push it will help to push us forward.

The (Re)connection Model was developed and first introduced in the Hoge Kempen National Park. This innovative project has attracted national and international attention and won awards. However, initially, people didn't want it in their own backyards. The Model was conceived of in Limburg, an area of NE Belgium where people historically made their livings from mining. Large parts of the economy had collapsed, and tens of thousands of people lost their jobs when mining came to an end. New ways of making a living had to be found. A few of us dreamed about finding a way to do this that would also help nature. It seemed like an impossible idea…

However, two unlikely partners reached an agreement in 1990 that turned out to be the first step on the road to change. A private Belgian nature conservation organisation, Natuurreservaten – now Natuurpunt – together with the mining company Kempische Steenkoolmijnen NV worked with government to create a nature reserve, the Regionaal Landschap Kempen en Maasland vzw (RLKM), of which I am director. It was nothing special, were it not for the fact that the founders were seemingly each other's opposites: a nature organisation and an industrial organisation. It was to be an extraordinarily successful marriage.

Following the example of the German 'Naturparken', the French 'Parcs naturels régionaux' and the English 'Areas of Outstanding Natural Beauty' that were developed to safeguard high-quality natural heritage landscapes, we in Limburg did not want to be left behind. The Regionaal Landschap Kempen en Maasland is characterised – like large parts of the province of Limburg – by a high number of large natural areas, beautiful heritage-rich and nature-rich landscapes and high levels of biodiversity. As a regional partnership in which all stakeholders in the Regionaal Landschap wanted to make a difference and it makes it clear and visible to everyone that investing in a heritage-rich natural landscape makes a substantial contribution to the regional economy and could be (part of) the solution after the mine closures. An idea of idealistic dreamers who don't know how the economy really works, the critics said.

A first major success was achieved in 1995 with the conception and development of the now internationally acclaimed 'Fietsroutenetwerk' (Cycle Route Network) that threads its way through the natural and heritage-rich landscape. This success convinced people that 'nature is sexy'. In 1997, the Hoge Kempen National Park was conceived, developed and established and in 2006 it was given the official status of Belgium's first national park. At the same time two high-quality additional cross-border landscape parks were established: the GrensPark Kempen~Broek and the RivierPark Maasvallei.

The Hoge Kempen National Park was the impetus that led to the development of the (Re)connection Model.[4] There would be no National Park without the insights and motivation of Johan Van Den Bosch, biologist, great thinker and designer, and Lambert Schoenmaekers, experienced landscape expert, and without the support of the entire RLKM team. They also made it possible to develop the (Re)connection Model, a plan that uses real-world experience to show that nature and the economy can make excellent partners and in the end there are no losers but only winners.

Much of what we dreamed of has come true. The experience has made us believe that we can step into the future with confidence. When I was awarded the Goldman Environmental Prize – known as the Green Nobel Prize – in San Francisco in 2008 for among other things the development of the Hoge Kempen National Park, there was suddenly a great deal of international interest in how we had accomplished it. We had an advantage on our side, namely the insights and efforts of the Flemish Agency for Nature and Forests, which had safeguarded large areas of protected nature since the middle of the last century. Based on their work a new chapter could be written with the Hoge Kempen National Park.

After many years of lobbying, we were able to convince policymakers to spend part of the reconversion funds – intended to rebuild the region after the mine closures – on restoring nature and developing Belgium's first national park. From the start of the first works in 2002, through 2006 when the new concept park opened, and until 2015, more than 100 million euros were invested and policymakers became increasingly convinced of the recruiting power of nature and the socio-economic added value of the park. The local community became intensely involved and enthused by the success of the national park.

---

4   The partners of the Hoge Kempen National Park are the real heroes. Without being able to be exhaustive, special thanks to the Flemish Agencies for Nature and Forests and Immovable Heritage, the municipalities, the provincial government of Limburg, the Flemish Region and all agencies and authorities involved, Tourism Flanders and Tourism Limburg, LRM, LISOM, LSM, Natuurpunt, Limburgs Landschap, PNC, Agricultural Sector, Entrepreneurs, University of Hasselt, Beekeepers, LIKONA... and all inhabitants, rangers, scouts and volunteers.

The region that had been disadvantaged by the mine closures sud-denly regained value. Soon people became proud of 'their' national park, and many felt reconnected to the land and the community. Nature was welcomed to stay, nature regained value for the community.

The park has 1.2 million visitors annually and an annual turno-ver of €191 million and has created 5,000 jobs. With relatively little convincing needed, an agreement was reached to increase the size of Hoge Kempen National Park in 2016 making it twice as big, twice as beautiful and twice as strong and successful ten years after its opening: the park has grown from 6,000 to 12,000 hectares. More than 110 million euros will be invested in the next five years.

This is exactly what the tree frog had taught me when I had looked him in the eye a few years earlier. Saving the world literally means that before you accuse world leaders and big corporates of not addressing the problems, you must get to work in your own backyard too – from NIMBY (Not In My Backyard) to PIMBY (Please In My Backyard). We have no right to ask others to protect the rainforest if we are failing to save our own region. We must do it ourselves. We must deliver a meaningful argument in an understandable language that engages and amazes people. In other words: we must practise what we preach. The (Re)connection Model offers a great opportunity for that.

An ethical and local response to global challenges

Opportunities abound when nature is seen as an ally and not an enemy, an ally that can provide people with an honourable and valu-able existence. The (Re)connection Model aims to restore and protect nature and develop or adjust recognisable natural spaces – such as national parks, for example – and (re)connect them to society and the local community. By focusing on the connection of people and nature, the model can equally inspire the development of cities and villages.

How exactly does the (Re)connection Model work? The whole world is looking for viable initiatives that can provide economic security and job security for local people while helping to revitalise nature. It is exactly this challenge that the Model is meeting. New initiatives will have to be organised in a nature-friendly, climate-robust, circular, regenerative, inclusive and socially balanced way. Not just because it would be desirable, but because it must be so. Too often nature is neatly locked up and trapped in nature reserves where it will perish without restoration, contact and exchange and help from us. In these cases, nature is seen as a cost and an inconvenient cost in times of setbacks when in fact nature can be part of the solution. It is time to liberate nature and give it back some space. By giving space to nature, we give space to ourselves.

The (Re)connection Model was designed to reconnect society with nature, to make the invisible visible again. It has high ambitions for nature. It treats nature as something that has value in an economic and ecological system. The need for space is central to the model. Natural heritage and ecosystem services are in directing and leading roles. The model offers a well-founded alternative to the countless nature-destroying ideas and projects that are still being floated every day to revitalise regions, such as new building projects, shopping malls and new recreational parks. Rarely is new space created or demolished in favour of nature. Yet demolition can be very constructive, a signal for recovery. Let me explain.

The power of the (Re)connection Model lies in reverse thinking whereby omissions or doing nothing creates added value. The goal is more quality with less quantity, where natural space and natural design are the guiding principles. The Model is designed as an open and Nature-Based Solution, which can be applied globally, with local answers providing outcomes for the global challenges of biodiversity loss, climate change and sustainable development while respecting cultural and religious backgrounds. Nature-based solutions use nature to solve social problems while helping the natural ecosystem.

The term *glocal* is used to describe the process of finding local solutions to global challenges, and is based on the Japanese word 'dochakuka' meaning global localisation. Since the 1990s, glocalisation has been theorised by various sociologists and social scientists. The process is based on the knowledge that global systemic change can only succeed through a chain of many connecting and mutually reinforcing local changes. A glocal model assumes the local to serve the global. Each level takes maximum account of the higher goals – in this case, the UN Sustainable Development Goals.

The Model is also anchored with the LATTE (Local, Authentic, Trustworthy, Traceable and Ethical) values and constructed according to them. LATTE values are derived from several trends that developed during the baby boom generation (people born between 1946-1964). LATTE values align very well with the Millennium Goals and the Sustainable Development Goals. They show that nature is the basis for 'everything'. An intact biosphere is thereby the prerequisite for a healthy society and a sustainable economy (as also shown in the figure on the next page).

A summary of the vision for the Model was that it must be locally anchored and connected to society, based on the authenticity of the region and faithfully and openly constructed. It should be traceable and transparent in word and deed, and ethically developed and realised. This fidelity to natural connections can be strong, as they are

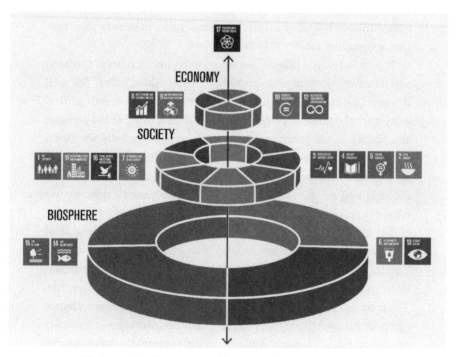

FIGURE: The intact biosphere as a condition for society and economy
SOURCE: Azote Images for Stockholm Resilience Centre

for example in Yellowstone National Park, in parts of the rainforest in Brazil and Ecuador or in Virunga National Park in Africa. The focus was on nature-based strengthening of human and political connections. Hence (Re) is written in brackets, i.e. (Re)connection. Nature helps us if we give it space to do so.

Power lines

The (Re)connection Model is fed by four lines of force; it is guided by three principles and there are four categories of results. We will examine each of these in detail. Starting with the lines of force – these create a foundation for the challenges we face locally and globally. And they must be set in motion by politicians, businesses and organisations, each of which wants to show leadership. And the beauty here is always that nature does not need convincing, it springs right along with this decisiveness. The four lines of force are:

Connecting nature with nature
Connecting people with nature
Connecting businesses with nature
Connecting policy and practice

(Re)connecting nature with nature

It all starts with giving back to nature what belongs to nature. Restoring, building out and buffering and managing robust nature forms the backbone of the Model, and includes actions such as legally anchoring new spaces for nature, rewilding projects, reintroducing species, closing or (partially) breaking up roads (softening), building nature bridges or tunnels (defragmentation) restoring and strengthening natural infrastructure, demolishing and converting industrial zones, demolishing buildings and enclaves that are not in line with nature objectives, changing land use and giving space back to rivers. The Model aims to give back to nature what belongs to nature.

The ecological results of our flood protection programme are spectacular: in the past 30 years, the space for nature has doubled and biodiversity has tripled.

The Model also aims to restore, connect and make visible again existing and sometimes forgotten nature. Creating new space for nature is not easy, often because official spatial plans must be revised or adjusted. In regions where nature is fragmented – as in large parts of western Europe – reconnecting nature is essential to form a robust whole within which natural processes can sustain themselves. Projects like these demonstrate the resilience of nature as well as that of the stakeholders and politicians involved. It takes courage and conviction to decide to extinguish active industrial zones or convert construction zones and recreation zones into nature zones. Within the (Re)connection Mode the option of developing 'new nature' becomes feasible and the benefits are made visible.

There are great examples of connecting nature with nature. An interesting approach is to apply the work-with-work method or to organise green neighbourhoods. In green post-development, an area with a temporary zoning is given a permanent and green spatial destination. Temporary zoning is for temporary activities such as the extraction of sand, loam, gravel or clay. In the work-with-work method, the ideal final image for nature is included in the plans. Think of developing and restoring habitats during reclamation works or river widening works. By applying this methodology, much less machinery needs to be used, nature disruption is reduced, and implementation costs decrease. Opportunities sometimes arise that are like gold for nature conservation. The Maas Valley River Park is a good example. To protect residents from flooding, a large-scale 'flood protection programme' for the Meuse River was set up in Belgium and the Netherlands. Combining flood protection with river widening and nature development created new opportunities for connections and the creation of new nature areas along the banks of the Meuse. The ecological results are spectacular: in the past 30 years, the space for nature has doubled and biodiversity has tripled.

(Re)connecting people with nature

The second line of force involves finding ways for people to make, restore or improve their physical and mental connection with nature. How can we make ourselves and others aware of what nature is, how nature functions, how we are part of it, what (health) benefits nature offers us and how we should interact with it? In this way, nature does not start in a nature reserve, but in our heads and in our flowerpots on the windowsill; it happens at your back door and in your street. Education is essential to facilitate these connections, in all shapes and colours, for all ages, for everyone. Anchoring with the local community is central to this and should involve the residents, the partners and entrepreneurs involved, as well as the local politicians. Nature is the first beneficiary of the Model, but the people and the partners will harvest the first fruit and can act as enthusiastic ambassadors.

> Nature does not start in a nature reserve, but in our heads and in our flowerpots on the windowsill. It happens at your back door and in your street.

The (Re)connection Model considers the local culture and analyses potential bottlenecks and opportunities, integrates needs and provides a transparent view of the challenges of a large nature project. The Model tries to paint a picture of expectations, opportunities for tourism and local business. It shows what jobs can be created and how and where to welcome residents and visitors. In all these ways, the (Re)connection Model can be a source of inspiration in regional and urban development.

The Model is based on a bottom-up approach that involves the local community and local stakeholders in the development process. Surprisingly, a lot of useful knowledge is still available within these local communities, left unused by larger organisations and policy makers, but from which much can be learned. Local customs can be introduced into conservation management; stories and legends can help to set up a line of communication between your organisation and the local community. By actively involving these customs and stories in the development process and introducing local communities to the benefits of protecting nature, support for nature increases noticeably.

Consequently, this approach is not time-consuming in the long run, but rather time-saving. And the bottom-up approach is often simply great fun as well.

The connection between nature and people is strengthened by developing a 'strong brand' including a recognisable corporate image, by creating well located visitor centres and park entrances and by an innovative education programme. National Parks and UNESCO sites are among the best-known 'strong brands' in the world and stand for quality. But regional landscapes, landscape parks, river parks, border parks or larger nature reserves can also be or become strong brands.

(Re)connecting businesses with nature

The third line of force is about the role that business must play. If we want to restore nature, we will have to transition to a circular or even regenerative economy. In other words, an economy that gives back more than what it takes and does justice to nature, seeing nature as part and partner. For this, we desperately need innovative and co-creating entrepreneurs. This does not just mean the business angels or CEOs of large companies, but also the social entrepreneurs, the small business owners and the self-employed. Finally, we need to propose viable ways for farmers to become involved in nature-inclusive and regenerative agriculture.

Connecting businesses and nature takes place at different levels. Increasingly, businesses are engaging by taking nature into account, exploring nature-inclusive working conditions and evolving towards circularity. By literally bringing nature close to the local community – by locating park entrances there, for example, or by creating green links – local entrepreneurs can fully benefit from additional customer potential that the Model can provide, and they will increasingly align themselves with the park entrance; a 'natural' advantage. Some preparation is required. The arrival of a national park, for example, can make the difference between mere economic survival and being profitable for some businesses near the park. Both the baker and the butcher, the B&B operator, the local café and the local wine merchant or potter benefit directly from the new nature link.

The local farmer can get his share of the benefits of the park through the sale of locally produced regional and organic products. This gets a flywheel turning. Other companies will then adapt their product range and donate part of the proceeds for the protection of nature or an endangered species.

Projects from other regions also inspired the (Re)connection Model. There are many examples. 'Bean to Bar bar Virunga', a project by Belgian Dominique Persoone, is one of them. The chocolate is made by local farmers and part of the proceeds go to Virunga National Park. Small steps can become big steps and big multinationals are also playing their part in the transition. When developing the Hoge Kempen National Park, SIBELCO – an internationally renowned Belgian quartz sand company – was willing to relocate the company headquarters and local factory nine years before its business plan expired so that their site could be developed as part of the national park.

(Re)connecting policy with practice

The fourth line of force is that of governments, businesses, civil society organisations, scientists and citizens like you and me taking action and putting ideas into practice. A government with a visionary policy is important. First and foremost, it is about public policy, but this necessary force is not limited to government. It is a job we must do together: businesses, organisations, scientists and everyone who wants to play a role to develop a vision that fits today's reality, both locally and far beyond our borders. The policies of companies and organisations of all kinds are decisive for a sustainable transition. Increasingly, companies are willing to apply and integrate nature-based solutions into their business philosophy and are willing to co-invest. New businesses and existing local businesses are producing sustainable and organic local products (food, drinks, local crafts), creating an interesting new niche: the wildlife economy.

In addition, scientific research institutes and universities have an important role to play because policy choices are (should be) based on scientific insights and evaluations. A good example is the GrensPark Kempen~Broek on the border between Flanders and the Netherlands.

For more than 20 years all stakeholders have been working together as a true area coalition, taking initiatives to develop a landscape park. Tens of millions of euros were invested in restoring nature and creating a natural climate buffer, with positive results both for biodiversity and for residents and local entrepreneurs. So, it was not difficult for the stakeholders to put a new policy intention into practice and develop a cross-border UNESCO Man and Biosphere area.

In nature, everything interacts with everything else for the betterment of all. Nature helps us survive if we help nature survive. New economic thinking involves the same form of cooperation that is so natural to nature. The (Re)connection Model works from that integral and integrative area-based vision. Its strength lies in the totality and togetherness of the participating parties and regional stakeholders. Within this strong area coalition, cooperation with the various levels of government is crucial. Together for more nature, together for better nature and together for resilient nature. With both the United Nations and the European Union imposing obligations and systems on member states to halt the decline of and restore biodiversity, governments are being urged to take responsibility.

The (Re)connection Model is the guarantor for achieving the international goals and translating them into local and regional policies. Universities, colleges and research institutes are asked to carry out and report on scientific analyses to further develop the international-scientific connection and provide new training if necessary. For the Hoge Kempen National Park, for instance, a collaboration has been set up with Hasselt University, which includes the development of an International Field Study Centre (FRC UHasselt) and the Ecotron. The Ecotron – part of the Field Research Centre – is a large scale research infrastructure that allows for sophisticated state-of-the-art controlled climate experiments to study the effects of climate, and climate change on ecosystem functioning. It provides insight into the impact of climate on a given ecosystem that cannot be gained by field experiments (which are often too complex) or in controlled laboratory experiments (which are often too reductive).

So, we need to connect nature with nature, humans with nature, businesses with nature and put all that into practice, together. To

do that, we need to consider principles underlying the (Re)connec-
tion Model.

The underlying principles of the (Re)connection Model

In addition to the lines of force above, there are three principles that
are important to the (Re)connection Model and act as preconditions
that must be met for the lines of force to be set in motion. Below, I
discuss those principles:
1 The carrying capacity of nature
2 Smart zoning
3 An integrated and inclusive approach

Carrying capacity of nature

Nature is the leading principle of the (Re)connection Model, based
on its carrying capacity as determined by the number of species or
plants or animals in a suitable habitat. If there is too much disturbance,
the carrying capacity and the natural balance is destabilised, which
can cause species to disappear. Preventing the carrying capacity from
being exceeded is a priority principle that influences policy choices. If
there is too much natural pressure in terms of visitor numbers and if
the infrastructure cannot support a particular capacity the investment
or activity is abandoned, and alternatives are sought.

For example, if too many visitors in a particular habitat is demon-
strably leading to the disappearance of critical or rare species, then the
footpath will be moved, or the habitat closed to the public. The principle of guiding and directing nature is called the Sandford Principle,
after Lord Sandford who chaired the National Parks Policy Review
Committee of England and Wales between 1971 and 1974. He argued
that in conflicting situations, nature goals should take precedence.
Thus, nature determines what is possible.

Smart zoning

Besides the carrying capacity of nature, we need to think about what we can do where. The way in which we spatially classify the environment is crucial for success. We distinguish three zones that are intertwined and connected:
- Impact zone
- Focus zone
- Core zone

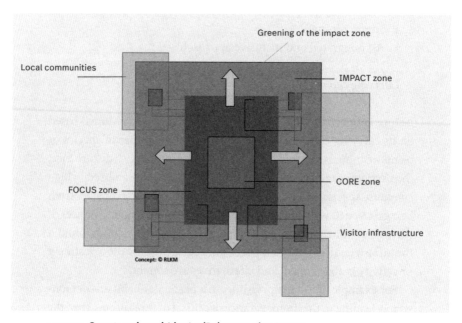

FIGURE: *Smart zoning within the (Re)connection Model*

The impact zone

When developing large nature reserves and large natural parks, merely protecting the area by itself is not enough because the environmental impact and outside influences are too great and too direct. Think of eutrophication, pollution, urbanisation and residential pressure to the edges, overpressure by recreation and so on (*negative outside-in*). It is therefore important to define a wide impact zone within the sphere of influence. This impact zone can even be more than double the size of the focus zone. On the other hand, natural values and influences can have a strong positive impact from the core and focus zones, and impact zones can play an important connecting role for people and nature (*positive inside-out*). Consider greening such as the creation of wooded borders and tree rows, stream restoration, etc. that are extended into the village or town centre. In the impact zone, other functions, such as living and working, can be present, with attention to both nature and economic activity.

By working with an impact zone, signage, promotion and communication can be aligned more strongly and broadly, making the visibility and sphere of influence of the area or park much greater. Additional opportunities can be developed with partners and stakeholders a bit further away from the park. In addition, the smaller natural areas and parks within the impact zone can be involved and strengthen their connection to the park or area in the focus zone.

The focus zone and the core zone

The focus zone and the core zone together form a recognisable ecological-landscape functioning whole of the area or park. The core zones are the spatial and legally regulated nature destinations defined in the land use plans such as a nature or forest reserve or a European Natura 2000 site. Additional nature protection measures can be applied within core zones. In Germany, for example, some zones can be demarcated and no human activity or management is allowed within them. Here, the rule 'leave nature to nature' ('Natur Natur sein lassen') applies. The aim is to stop managing 3% of all nature in Germany and steer away from rewilding processes, allowing only purely natural processes, sometimes combined with the reintroduction of large grazers. In the Hoge Kempen National Park, a core zone for scientific research has been designated, an area accessible only to scientists to investigate natural processes.

Focus zones are usually also legally regulated nature destinations, but they can be wider and combined with other functions, such as agriculture, for example, but they are nature-inclusive and fulfil a buffering and supporting function within the ecological-landscape whole. Within the core and focus zones, the Sandford principle of guiding and directing nature applies.

The park's visitor infrastructure – often called gateways – are located 'outside' the focus zone and within the impact zone near places where social and/or economic activity already takes place. In the Hoge Kempen National Park example, they are therefore located outside the official boundaries of the national park. By (re)locating visitor infrastructure outside the focus zone, many benefits can be added.

The entrance gate and visitor centres in about 85% of national parks worldwide are within the official boundaries of the national park. With all its consequences: overcrowding of (too many) visitors, litter and increased disturbance that often exceeds the carrying capacity of nature, and so on. Locating visitor infrastructure outside the focus zone and near village centres, for example, relieves pressure on nature, boosts the local economy and creates additional jobs.

Unlocking on a landscape scale

By locating visitor infrastructure outside the focus zone, nature pressure is relieved, the local economy is boosted and additional jobs are created.

Nature management organisations usually have rights only within the managed area or park. This means that the accessibility of, for example, footpaths, cycle paths and bridleways is organised within the core nature reserve. After all, the public rightly expects accessibility. Whether in the Hoge Veluwe or in many areas of Natuurpunt in Flanders or national parks in the US, accessibility is always organised internally. That seems logical because they own or manage it and can therefore decide for themselves. Outside the borders, this is often not possible at all. As a result, recreational access there is much less organised or not organised at all. This has a potentially negative impact on nature, as accessibility is concentrated entirely within the area one wants to protect for nature and its species. In other words, greater concentration of visitors exceeds the carrying capacity of nature, resulting in a possible drastic decline of nature and its species.

People are much more likely to stay in less vulnerable places if they are aware of the vulnerability of nature, and if access is cleverly organised and placed outside the official boundaries of the owned or managed area. This distributes the pressure of visitor numbers and protects the carrying capacity of nature. It is precisely for this reason that all visitor infrastructure is best located 'outside' the national park and all recreational access is then organised 'on a landscape scale', spread over a much larger area than just the national park. This approach allows for interesting solutions and has great advantages for combinations with hospitality, culture, heritage. The combination of smart access to the most beautiful places outside the national park increases the park's attractiveness. Engagement remains high and the overall area can handle many more visitors without additional nature disturbance and without lowering the carrying capacity. So, there are many gains to be made and the carrying capacity of nature can be eased considerably by organising the recreational infrastructure at the landscape level, both inside and outside the focus zone. The objective is to decrease intrusions by humans in areas where the vulnerability of nature increases.

The park entrances, located outside the focus zones, are landmarks and act as attractive information points and transfer points to the park. The entrances are not only the starting point for a walking or cycling tour, but they also offer basic information about the area or park, combined with an additional (thematic) experience such as, for example, an insect museum, a planetarium, a castle or ruin. Because of the attraction, the experience, the natural environment and the connection to the park, visitors often linger at the entrance gates.

Lieteberg, the site of an entrance to Hoge Kempen National Park, is a great example. A popular attraction, the 'barefoot trail', is located there, just outside the boundary of the park. Visitors walk barefoot for two hours along a fantastic nature trail, finishing in a nearby café with a Trappist beer and a piece of flan. This attraction receives 140,000 visitors each year. Those visitors all come to the national park but only a fraction enter the boundaries of the national park itself. The attraction is enough for most. Through this clever zoning, we reduce human pressure on nature without making people feel short-changed.

Paid or free access?

Whether people should be entitled to free or paid access to nature needs critical consideration. Just think of national parks in the US or the Hoge Veluwe National Park in the Netherlands or other private parks. In purely fee-paying parks, costs and benefits can be evaluated more easily, but the risk of exclusion for the lowest-income classes is high. In freely accessible parks, the nature experience is offered freely to everyone, and the risk of exclusion is lower. The nature-for-all / all-for-nature principle, which does not exclude any target group, is obviously most desirable for social balance.

Integrated and inclusive approach

The third principle is to have an integrated and inclusive approach. You know that it is ultimately you and I who determine what is and what is not valuable. We should determine value from the perspective of knowledge and the inclusive integrated perspective. Just as the value of Vincent van Gogh's *Sunflowers* is not determined by the cost of the paint and the canvas, a forest is not valued by the amount of wood it contains.

The same logic applies to an alpine meadow or other natural eco-systems; their value can be based on the integrated value of all the services they provide to us. That is the power of the (Re)connection Model. It is not an isolated nature project, separate from local society, but an inclusive and social project, where all aspects are studied and addressed in an integrated way. See figure below.

The Model can be used to test the likelihood of success for new projects. Projects can be evaluated against several fixed parameters, including – importantly – if the carrying capacity of nature is leading and normative (i.e. it meets a local need), and an estimate is made of its chances of success. Once a project is selected, building blocks are provided that – like a Rubik's cube – allow for maximum integration and connection.

Results: fourfold return

Finally, in addition to the four lines of force and the three principles, there are four result fields. What does the model deliver? The model can deliver some very remarkable outcomes. For instance, big returns can be made from investments in natural capital, in the form of more biodiversity and more healthy ecosystems. Investments in natural capital also increase social capital. The economy is stimulated, jobs are created, and people connect in more and better ways. Human capital increases in value through investments in natural capital. People rediscover the health value of nature and learn to make themselves useful in new ways, there is an increase in knowledge exchange, people feel inspired, there is an increase in social diversity which results in multicultural benefits. Finally, there is an attractive economic return on these investments with increasing (new) financial flows and with much more local investment and benefits. The cumulative effects will remove any doubts about success. It is self-evident that nature will benefit as protection levels and restoration opportunities increase. It is important to show how investing in nature benefits human capital and social capital. Making the return-on-investment visible increases support from decision makers, the involved authorities, various target groups and the public. The numbers speak for themselves to the degree that investment is an obvious choice, a 'no-brainer'.

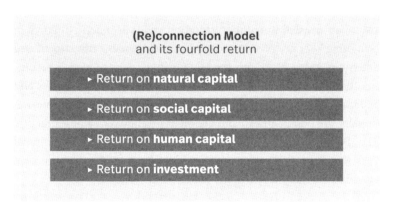

FIGURE: *Integrated & Inclusive Approach (Re)connection Model*

A cost-benefit analysis was done for Hoge Kempen National Park in 2010. The result was the sum of the costs for and benefits from storage of CO2, costs savings for drinking water, the national park's tourism revenue, the extra income from trade around the national park, the avoided costs and healthcare revenue, the extra revenue from VAT and other government taxes, the extra revenue from real estate around the national park, the direct nature revenue (wood and heather mowing) and the attributable share of business turnover. The result demonstrated that that park was a great success, and it has remained a success over the years.

Nature Bank is the best bank in the world

Total direct and indirect revenues related to the Hoge Kempen National Park (2009) were estimated at €191 million and 5,000 jobs were created. The return on investment was about one to ten: every euro invested generated ten euros for the local community. Impressive, right? We can prove that integrated and inclusive investment in nature produces positive results and is a catalyst for regional development. During my time as president of EUROPARC Federation I saw many other nature parks – inside and outside Europe – achieving similar results.

Metsähallitus, Parks & Wildlife Finland, surveyed 41 Finnish national parks and came up with similar results. And UNEP, the environmental branch of the United Nations, concluded in its recent study *Beyond GDP: making nature count in the shift to sustainability* (2022) that every US dollar invested in nature restoration yields as much as USD 30 in economic benefits. Nature projects are a sustainable investment and a hefty incentive with impressively positive socio-economic results. In other words, nature is the best bank in the world. The success and experiences of the (Re)connection Model are being studied internationally, are being applied and are often promoted as a best practice. The (Re)connection Model and the way the Hoge Kempen National Park was developed and set up formed the basis for the establishment of additional national parks in Flanders and Wallonia.

New funding models

Experience with the (Re)connection Model shows that we need to be honest about what we calculate and how we calculate it. The Model has been duplicated in different parks around the world showing that our success is reproducible. The biodiversity loss and climate crises are symptomatic of a collapsing planet. Awareness is rising; just about everyone feels that something needs to be done. Yet a balanced budget seems to be more important than a planet out of balance, even when it leads to billions of euros and dollars being literally washed away. Party interests still take precedence over the common good, and electoral gains get more attention than existential issues. Everyone calls for responsibility, but no one feels empowered. Thinking things through like this, it seems inevitable that we will lose the essential functions that make life possible. Our planet will survive no matter what, with or without humans. We, on the other hand, will not survive without a healthy and resilient planet.

Should we simply accept that our grandchildren will never see an elephant or a skylark, except in picture books? Should we just learn to adapt to the consequences of a collapsing planet that is growing ever warmer? Or can we still turn the tide? What is certain is that this decade will be decisive for the future of humanity and all the inhabitants on our planet.

There are about four million different species of animals and plants in the world. They have all devised their own solutions and survival strategies to stay alive. Our encroachment into nature's space and the impact of our pollution have put one million species at risk of extinction this century. One million survival strategies gone, forever. With the disappearance of life forms, our natural ecosystems that provide us with clean air, clean water, healthy food and health every day will also vanish.

Our management of the coronavirus pandemic showed that we are capable of rapid action, locally and internationally; we collaborated and developed a vaccine three times faster than expected. Perhaps most importantly, politicians heeded the advice of scientists – the virologists and epidemiologists – and based their policy actions on it. A solution did not seem feasible nor affordable, but money was suddenly no obstacle when the need for a solution become so obvious and so many lives were at risk. Despite some opposition on social media, we achieved a great deal together. We changed our behaviour radically. It taught us that change is possible if we have no other choice.

Yet for now, the coronavirus approach stands in stark contrast to attempts to tackle the biodiversity and climate crisis. Perhaps more of us need to see and feel the pain before we feel compelled to take action. A coronavirus infection could have led to death in a matter of days, while the devastating consequences of climate change and biodiversity loss has, until now, happened slowly over decades. But the ultimate consequences of this will be infinitely greater than what we experienced during the pandemic. The uncomfortable truth is that the consequences of the coronavirus pandemic will be dwarfed by the destructive power of ecosystem loss and global warming.

We must evaluate our place on earth, do our arithmetic anew and more fairly. Financing the necessary systemic transition is feasible and affordable if we manage to re-believe in a new sustainability story, away from the buzz words of sustainability, and moving not in words but in action. It can be done, and it starts with restoring and protecting nature. Saving the tree frog is saving ourselves. We must make the now invisible value of ecosystem services visible in the calculation of the strength of a country's economy. This change would be a powerful lever to activate a systemic transition.

The costs of financing (the restoration of) natural ecosystems are negligible compared to the returns they already bring to us through ecosystem services. Yet, for the time being, we are failing to correct the planetary imbalance. Many still stubbornly assume that natural ecosystem services are infinite AND free. We are now being presented with the bill for years of neglect and for the destruction of nature. Our debt is mounting fast, in money and in human lives. How can we do things differently, what financing models should we adopt to do things differently?

I have referred to the value of natural ecosystems. By now you must be curious about what that value is. It is perplexing to note that this value has been denied for decades:

The Australian National University estimates the average value of all ecosystem services on Earth was USD 145 trillion per year in 1997 dropping to USD 125 trillion per year in 2011. Those are numbers with a lot of zeros. It bears repeating: the estimated loss of global eco-services from 1997 to 2011 due to land use change is $20.2 trillion per year… By way of contrast, I can immediately offer you another dazzling set of numbers, one with a rather different outcome: the economic return of Natura 2000 – the European network of nature reserves – is estimated at 200-300 billion euros a year. More than 4 million jobs are linked to these nature reserves. The up to 2.2 billion visits made to these areas each year generate between 5 billion and 9 billion euros. Every. Single. Year.

People are not just part of nature, people love nature. Research in 2015 by Cambridge University found that 8 billion visits are made to protected natural areas worldwide every year. Those visits bring in money, a lot of money. The annual total spending of all these visitors is estimated at USD 600 billion. A similar story can be told for the US. In 2020, 237 million people visited the 423 national park sites. Their spending was estimated at USD 14.5 billion and supported 234,000 jobs. These are visitor-related figures only. In 2011 the value of ecosystem services from national parks in the US was estimated at USD 98 billion a year. The economic return of the Hoge Kempen National Park in Belgium is estimated at 191 million euros per year supporting 5,000 jobs (people). A study of Finland's 40 national parks showed that every euro invested in a national park generates 10 euros for the local community.

The numbers, as it is said, do not lie. The value of ecosystem services is much more than the approximately USD 10 billion spent on protecting nature worldwide. We need to change our financial climate and our priorities.

Israeli historian and futurologist Professor Yuval Noah Harari, world-renowned for his bestselling books *Sapiens, Homo Deus* and *21 Lessons for the 21st Century*, believes it is not that difficult and not too late to combat climate change. In a recent interview with *The New York Times*, Harari argued that the challenge lies in recruiting the will to finance the fight against climate change and the loss of biodiversity. We need to decide which story we want to believe in. By Harari's estimate, the cost to avert catastrophic climate change is only two percent of GDP; 'Two per cent of GDP doesn't sound very impressive, and that's exactly what it's about. It is hopeful. So, it's not that we need to turn the whole economy around and start living in caves again. We just need to shift two percent of the budget.'

It is inevitable that we must make choices to achieve a sustainable society. We must end the procrastination. The inability of policy makers to reach agreement on strong policies and invest in nature is incomprehensible and irresponsible. An investment in nature is an investment in progress, over and above the need to solve the climate problem or the loss of natural ecosystems. The incalculable human misery and the financial burden of an out-of-control climate and the biodiversity crisis are many times greater than the cost of addressing these issues today. The costs of the climate disasters we can still avoid are savings we can invest in a sustainable future. So, I wholeheartedly agree with Harari. We need to stay on message and focus on the big stories we all support, stories through which we can develop new strategies.

According to Harari, history is a succession of beliefs in new stories. Belief in new stories has allowed humanity to advance even though situations like war, disease and hunger have been the rule, not the exception. We must develop and believe in new stories about sustainable futures and guiding philosophies supported by local solutions. 'If we need to finance change, we need to change financing'. Let me share with you a few new models to finance change.

Climate investments outside the budget –
Intergenerational Planetary Loan

One way to create new opportunities together is to deal with our finances in a new way, in fact, the way we did during the coronavirus pandemic. The old thinking was that governments should be frugal with recurring expenditures like social security or education and that those expenditures should be paid for with current revenues. It should be no surprise that the reallocation of budgeted funds to saving the planet has led to protracted discussions. This hurdle was avoided during the pandemic by putting all coronavirus investments outside of the budget. The current planetary crisis requires urgent, rapid action. This should be enabled for financing our planet's recovery as well. Putting all climate investments 'outside' the budget would solve the financing problem immediately. One way to do this is via an Intergenerational Planetary Loan, like arranging a mortgage for a house purchase where you pay off the debt over time. Climate investments – and that includes restoring our natural ecosystems – could be organised in a similar way. Yes, it would be a very big loan.

Suppose the world community (UN) were to decide that (all) countries can take out a planetary loan and place it off-budget and – now comes the extra innovation – the debt would not need to be repaid in 30 or 50 years, but in 1,000 years. Paying back one thousandth every year is a lot easier than one-thirtieth or one-fiftieth: a planetary, intergenerational loan as a new financing mechanism. The borrower could be the International Monetary Fund (IMF) or the World Bank because both have existing systems and processes to administer huge loans. As a matter of fact, the innovation lies in clever combinations and variations of some known methods. A precedent is the Netherlands, where long-term, intergenerational loans have been used for house purchases and off-budget investment was recently used globally to finance solutions for the coronavirus pandemic.

Another idea for a funding mechanism: the global community could take out 'Planetary Perpetuals' specifically for states (Perpetual subordinated loan). The borrower pays a perpetual stream of income to the lender in respect of interest due. The principle has no maturity date, i.e., it is never paid off. To keep everything on track and monitor efficiency, a Climate Agency could be set up within the UN.

Saving ourselves and the planet will not succeed within the short-term objectives and policies of the current economic system. More and more economists are advocating an 'out of the box' approach. Disentangling the desperately needed investment in nature outside of annual budget discussion is a simple and powerful measure that could be applied immediately. The methodology for arranging and administering a loan already exists, so what is stopping us?

There are alternative ideas on how to tackle the climate problem. The down-to-earth and visionary ideas of Dutch Marjan Minnesma, for example, are very appealing. The business expert, lawyer and phi-losopher became a leading force in the drive for an energy transition in the Netherlands in the first decades of this century. As co-founder (2007) of the Urgenda foundation Minnesma became known for her initiatives to accelerate the transition to an energy-neutral society. In the Netherlands, Urgenda calculated how many wind turbines and solar panels would be needed to meet energy needs in 2030. Their esti-mate was, in addition to large-scale wind farms in the North Sea and geothermal heat, the Netherlands energy needs would be fulfilled by 3,500 land-based wind turbines (3-4 MW) and 150 million solar panels. Urgenda's story is not only appealing, but it also makes the transition manageable. Assuming 380 municipalities in the Netherlands, only nine wind turbines per municipality would be needed. If one munic-ipality would erect more than nine, another municipality could erect eight. In this way, natural areas could reasonably be spared. As for the 150 million solar panels; that would be nine panels per person. If the farmer around the corner would put 200 panels on his barn, a monument could be spared. Urgenda simply shows that every effort makes sense.

Another financing option is the net zero home, also devised in the Netherlands. A net zero house generates as much – or more – energy than it consumes. These energy neutral homes offer residents major savings on energy costs. An energy bill of just a few cents per year or even a zero-euro energy bill is easy to achieve. There are other examples of similar initiatives in the Netherlands. Just as spectacular, for example, is the development of the Lightyear car. It runs almost entirely on solar energy and needs 70% less energy to recharge than other electric cars. A solution without charging stations, harnessing the sun as a free ecosystem service.

A Green Tax Shelter and the voluntary carbon market

A green initiative of a completely different order but no less interesting is the Green Tax Shelter, a concept analogous to an existing and pop-ular tax shelter in Belgium for audio-visual productions and the per-forming arts, plus another for start-ups. Belgian or foreign companies with operations in Belgium can enjoy significant tax benefits when investing in European audio-visual productions or the performing arts, provided several conditions are met. The tax benefit consists of a tax exemption of up to 310% on vested (not the promised) investments. There is also a Tax Shelter for start-ups whereby individuals can get a tax reduction in personal income tax of 30 or 45% if they acquire new shares directly from a start-up company or through a crowdfunding platform. Surely it cannot be difficult to develop a Green Tax Shelter for the acquisition and restoration of natural ecosystems. Nature would be restored; businesses and individuals would be happy. Who or what is stopping us?

Or how about rapidly scaling up a voluntary carbon market? There is growing interest in starting CO_2 reduction projects on a national scale through the voluntary carbon market. This trade is expected to grow rapidly. More and more companies, governments and citizens are actively working to reduce their own carbon footprint. CO_2 excesses can be dealt with by purchasing certificates in projects that reduce CO_2 emissions. Natural ecosystems can store and maintain significant amounts of CO_2. There is an urgent need to restore and expand these natural ecosystems, including the restoration of peatlands, planting of forests and so on. Carbon sequestration in soils is also an opportunity within regenerative agriculture. The Taskforce on Scaling Voluntary Carbon Markets (TSVCM), led and supported by luminaries from the world of finance and sponsored by the International Institute for Finance (IIF), is developing a new framework for voluntary carbon markets. In time, projects could also receive ISO certification (ISO14064). What is holding us back?

Earth on the stock market

One last point. Proposing Earth as the ultimate 'economic' weapon was something I had suggested once during a public debate. Other innovative thinkers have also philosophised about the same idea. Jan Van Den Bossche was the first to think of listing Earth on the stock market, for which I offer many thanks. As you are reading this book, you know that Earth is warming at a hellish rate, biodiversity is declining at a staggering rate and if we do nothing about it, we will find ourselves in a catastrophic mess of a situation. Despite this, urgent and drastic measures are failing to materialise. If Climate and Nature get any attention at all, it is as an afterthought and the pause button is pressed. Other concerns are given precedence: the coronavirus, the financial and energy crises, the Russian invasion of Ukraine, the death of the Queen, the World Cup in Qatar … Climate and nature are the eternal losers, something to worry about later.

Should we continue to pass responsibility to deal with the problem of climate change and biodiversity loss to the next generation? The agenda is set by stakeholders in the fossil fuel industries, agro-industry, carmakers, airlines, banking and other sectors. They have many accomplices: traders in doubt, lobby groups that block important interventions, trolls and dubious scientists who discharge contradictory information, whilst the popular media avoids the topic as much as possible. They are the weapon of those who wish to maintain the status quo.

Most politicians dare not go against the interests of those in power and hide behind a belief in ecomodernism, where we just continue to consume and hope that science and technology will solve it. Our officials hide behind the rant of 'lack of support'. We are kept sweet with the occupational therapy of non-fundamental actions, or we are saddled with individual guilt if our ecological footprint turns out to be too high. Small changes in personal behaviour unfortunately do not lead to the fundamental change that we need.

We can break through the destructive power of market-led thinking only by upending the dominant system. A profound change of direction only comes about through public debate and collective struggle. In this, nature and climate can no longer be pushed to the background, they must be at the table with us and demand that their limits and their rights be honoured.

A common concern for the place where we live is a new form of solidarity between people and nature. Suppose we list Earth on the stock market and turn the 8 billion Earth inhabitants into Earth shareholders? The stock market is nothing more than a kind of giant gambling game, with often pernicious consequences for Earth. The market relies on perception, the delusion of the moment. Let us throw

Earth and its future into the market in the form of Earth shares. With the commitment and promise to give both Earth and our future generations back a sustainable future.

A share in Earth costs one euro. You buy one or as many as you want or can. You can also buy Earth shares for other Earthlings who are less wealthy. That way, you make them co-owners of Earth and their future. In exchange for your Earth shareholding, you commit yourself to giving your loved ones and your 8 billion fellow Earthlings a promising future. Governments, companies, associations, schools and sponsors can purchase multiple shares which they distribute to less wealthy people. As an Earth shareholder, you must try to reduce your CO_2 emissions – not only individually, but also by exerting influence in the circles in which you find yourself (work, neighbourhood, association, etc.). The goal is to put 8 billion Earth shares on the market and make every inhabitant co-owner of the Earth and its future. To issue the Earth shares, we cooperate with Nature Bank, the world's most profitable bank, and we invest the collected capital in new projects.

The above examples of this chapter show that natural ecosystems are the best banking institution in the world. If we manage to develop regenerative economics and restore, reconnect and protect these existential natural ecosystems, they will deliver perpetual high returns. The systemic transition to a healthy planet really does not have to cost that much. Two percent of global GDP would go a long way. The healing of people and our planet is similar. Healthy people have a thousand wishes, sick people only one. People will do anything to regain their health. At any cost. A healthy planet fulfils many human wishes, a sick planet perhaps none. The choice is ours.

In this chapter, I have shown that we must begin to value nature and include it in calculating national budgets. I have shown how incredibly valuable a role nature plays in our economy and how we can and must recognise and compensate nature for that. The (Re)connection Model offers a practical and effective way to both distinguish and integrate ecology and the economy, to the degree

The (Re)connection Model amplifies the reality and the need to give nature a place in our economic thinking. It shows that taking action can be a profitable win-win situation for all.

that they reinforce one another. The Model amplifies the reality and the need to give nature a place in our economic thinking. It presents a new way of thinking and suggests actions we can take at the level of the government, business and as individuals. It shows that taking action can be a profitable win-win situation for all.

The (Re)connection Model is one way that we can give nature a place in our economic thinking. I have also mentioned other practical government measures that were creatively taken up by individuals, and where we appear to be able to work towards an economy that is truly sustainable and truly cares for nature.

In the next chapter, I would like to take you further into what you can do to save nature and make it a part of a collective effort by countries, governments, organisations, businesses and people like you and me.

Chapter 4

"I am the river – the river is me."

– A Whanganui Māori saying

WHAT CAN WE DO?

Give nature back its rights

The previous chapters have summarised the facts and figures of the ecological problems faced by our planet and the threat posed to all our planet's inhabitants, including us. If we do not act immediately, we know the prognosis – the disastrous collapse of biodiversity and the catastrophic effects of global warming. I have explained why our way of consuming, travelling and living, combined with the practices of industry and agriculture will make our planet unliveable if we continue to ignore its cries for help.

I hope to have convinced you that in addition to governments and businesses taking action, we individuals must challenge ourselves to take meaningful steps to stem the growing loss of biodiversity and the burgeoning problem of climate change. We need to attack these problems with a level of conviction and resolute courage that 50 years ago put a man on the moon in one decade.

We must remind one another every day that a regenerative, circular, biodiverse, climate-friendly society will offer us a healthier, higher quality, more stable, more social and more sustainable way of life. I have tried to show you that the changes we need to make are within our reach. We have the scientific knowledge to show us the path to a healthier planet; the evidence on how to make a difference is available for leaders at the global and local level. They will simply need to start stepping out of the role of maintaining business as usual that the ones before them have assumed for too long.

I have proposed the (Re)connection Model, as an example of what can be achieved through a collaboration between scientists, conservationists, politicians and entrepreneurs who share the goal of improving ecology and the economy at the same time; that one can support the other. We can achieve improbably transformational results if we work together for the benefit of people and nature.

Our journey to success in saving our planet Earth begins with the realisation that nature has a price. Nature offers us unimaginable wealth without ever asking for anything in return. But nature's capacity to keep giving will soon reach its limits if we do not begin to pay nature back. We must take up our responsibility to pay nature back; we must respect nature's rights.

The rights of nature are the focus of this chapter. The human experience has been characterised by historical and contemporary struggles for universal rights and their enforcement for all inhabitants of our planet. Now it is nature's turn to assert its need for a set of universal rights and for UN Green Helmets, which I will come back to later on in this chapter, to protect those rights, just like the UN Blue Helmets protect the UN Human Rights.

In which language could a new story be written?

The twenty-first century began with a financial *meltdown*, a climatic *breakdown*, an ecological *shutdown* and a virological *lockdown*. We need systemic changes in how we function as a species, and we need to make these changes rapidly. Though it will be painful to adapt, if we do not make the necessary changes, the pain we will face in 20 years' time will be many orders of magnitude worse. Doing nothing will make the cost of recovery higher and the consequences much more severe.

To make these systemic changes possible, we need support and a persuasive and fact-based recruiting story – a love story for the planet – that will benefit everyone, without concealing underlying reasons or unpleasant truths. Many realise this, many also do not (yet) because they do not understand the complexities, challenges, nor the benefits and they do not recognise the love for humanity that lies behind our anxiety and frustration. This mismatch too often leads to resignation, disbelief, bitterness and a lack of support. There is a great need for people and organisations who can articulate, in understandable language, that restoring natural ecosystems pays off in the short and long term, both at the community and individual level, and at the economic and social level. We need to explain very clearly that a circular, regenerative, biodiverse, climate-friendly society is healthier, of better quality, stable, social and sustainable for our future, the future of society and of the planet. Once the existential value of a healthy environment can be understood, support and decision making will follow.

Experience gained over many decades of involvement in the debate about the environment shows that language has been a major stumbling block. Discussions about biodiversity loss and climate change are beset by problems, so whether the audience and the speaker are communicating in Dutch, English or Mandarin Chinese, the messages are often misunderstood. Language is far more than strings of words that deliver messages. Language can also convey sentiments and nuanced feelings, sometimes intentionally, sometimes not. For 30 years, I have struggled, fumbled, stumbled and marvelled at how difficult it is to find the right language, the right words, the right melody, the key to conveying messages that – to my ear and in my mind and heart – are patently obvious and clear. When speaking to an audience that already agrees with me, I can get the false sense that it is easy to deliver my message – until I realise that I am just preaching to the choir. How can I convince others? What words can I use? Business executives and politicians are more familiar with the language of economics than is an artist or a conservationist. A physician communicates completely differently from a housewife, and a farmer is more practical when discussing a harvest than a scientist is when discussing a theory (scientists seem to assume far too often that good theories are inherently practical).

Members of many disciplines are united by their own jargon or even their own worldview. Speakers from other disciplines must 'seduce' such audiences to encourage them to be receptive to the message. An alternative is to use 'general' or neutral language and not distinguish between different audiences and listeners. But this is done at the risk of losing the power of language to build connections? There is an immense difference between language and jargon, and between the language and the 'story'.

Studies demonstrate that messages composed of a story are more easily retained than messages without one, meaning that when one is trying to win over an audience it is best to avoid a dry enumeration of facts. Facts are often no match for the power of stories delivered with emotion, feelings and love. You will probably have experienced it yourself; you remember much less from a dry summation of facts than when they are presented as part of a good story. This is due to how we process and store information in our brain. Humans excel at retaining stories and anecdotes. We are less good at processing and remembering dry facts and figures.

Information processing has been the focus of an extraordinary amount of nuanced research but, in a nutshell, its relevance to my argument boils down to this: you may be surprised by how biased we are in the formation of memories from our experiences. Our recollection of events is usually incomplete, though we may think otherwise, and it is highly dependent on the feelings we had during the experience. Our brains retain stories, versus dry facts, in a specific way, referred to as the peak-end theory of memory processing. We cannot remember every fact or detail, so our brain uses mnemonics or mnemonic devices (tools to assist memory) to archive information. Our brain focuses subconsciously on two points in a story: the peak and the end. Our brain remembers the peak – which can be either positive or negative – and when the story reaches its end our brain archives these two points in long-term memory. Think about 9/11, for example. Everyone remembers the spike – two planes piercing the Twin Towers of the World Trade Center in New York in 2001, that many victims were trapped in stairwells, and we remember the international outrage and sadness.

Therefore, I must choose my story with extreme care when I want to express my love for the planet; it can make a world of difference. I have taken this into account as I spread the news about the (Re)connection Model. Language and stories have proven to be important tools to engage people and reconnect them to nature. Perhaps in the future artificial intelligence can help create new stories to connect us with one another. Tech giant Microsoft is a firm believer in this new technology and has invested USD 13 billion in it. You can simply ask ChatGPT, an AI chatbox, to gather and synthesise information and within seconds it will produce a report on its findings. Some work is needed to bring the system fully up to scratch, but a huge market awaits its full implementation. It will be valued at a minimum for providing inspiration when one is feeling less creative than usual or suffering from writer's block.

In any debate or discussion, if we want to make a point, we need to constantly explore and adapt the language we are using and the story we wrap around it. We may even need to learn or create new languages and stories as well as reinvigorating the ones we already know. I often find a starting point for new narratives by thinking about my own rights and those of others and how, as a logical consequence, we value our dependence on nature and our dependence on each other. That is where it can all begin.

Nature's rights

In our western way of thinking, humans are at the centre of everything, including our laws and regulations and, by extension, justice. In fact, animals are 'things' that we humans can own, like we own a car or a house. Nature is considered our property and as owners we have unlimited power over it. But this way of thinking is shifting. In contrast, people in several parts of the world think differently about nature and they are working on initiatives to give rights to nature itself.

Changes are being made to criminal and civil law. The new laws would allow nature to hold other legal entities privately liable for damage to nature in the same way that one can hold a motorist liable for collision with your car. But it will also be possible to hold the state, companies or individuals criminally liable on behalf of nature. Calls to criminalise 'ecocide' – the destruction of nature – are gaining strength.

Why should a tree, an ocean or a river not have rights? Denying nature its rights is simply an attitude and not an inalienable truth. Is it not time to change this? In these days of climate change, biodiversity loss and other ecological crises, this change in attitude and new laws that would come from this change could be a game-changer. Recognising the legal rights of nature would emancipate ecological systems. Instead of an anthropocentric society, we could be on the verge of adopting an ecocentric one. And why not? This approach would designate that the intrinsic value of all life is essential, as it has always been for many indigenous peoples. An ancient and an ultramodern idea, in other words. It would mean that, as humans, we would be legally responsible for our actions and we would be obligated to consider the legitimate interests of natural ecosystems, of all forms of life and of future generations. The possibility that nature could eventually claim its rights is not an idealistic fantasy, but a serious likelihood.

Nature claimed its rights in a remarkable action on 3 May 2019, at the Palace of Justice in Brussels. The court passed judgement on behalf of 82 trees as part of the Belgian climate lawsuit. The court was petitioned to recognise the trees themselves as co-owners, i.e., as legal entities with all the associated rights of such entities. For non-lawyers: an entity is a legal construction that allows an abstract entity or organisation to act as a fullyfledged and legally capable person having the rights and duties of a natural person. This is analogous to a company being a legal entity even though is not a flesh-and-blood human being. Eyebrows were raised and the trial was the butt of jokes on social media. Why should trees be treated as legal entities? Also, are more laws needed to protect nature?

Nature would not be in the state it is in today if there were already enough laws to protect it. Urban sprawl is destroying open space at breakneck speed. My corner of the world, Flanders in Belgium, is Europe's most fragmented region after Malta. 89% of all natural ecosystems in Flanders are contained within areas smaller than one hectare – postage stamp nature – and subject to enormous environmental pressure from outside. A not insignificant reason for this is the (legal) enclosure of nature in protected areas and the ever-increasing uptake of this land for exploitation at a rate of 5 hectares per day. Globally, more than 50% of the population lives in urban areas. By 2045, the world's urban population will increase 1.5 times, to 6 billion. According to the study *Rapid rise in urban sprawl: Global hotspots and trends since 1990*, published in 2022, urban sprawl increased by 95 per cent in 24 years. Built-up areas grew almost 4% each year, almost 28 km² per day, or 1.16 km² per hour.

This evolution obviously has major implications. From the UN *World Water Development Report* 2019, we learn that since the 1980s, global water consumption has increased by about 1% annually, due to a combination of population growth, socio-economic development and changing consumption patterns. Global water demand is expected to continue growing at the same rate until 2050, with an increase of 20-30% above current levels of water use, mainly due to rising demand in the industrial and domestic sectors. More than 2 billion people will then live in countries with high water stress and about 4 billion people will face severe water scarcity for at least one month a year. Stress levels will thus continue to rise as water demand increases and the effects of climate change intensify. Apparently, we manage to keep destroying nature even as we criminalise nature violations.

Perhaps it is instructive to look over the wall here, at common legal practices in the world of business. Why does a business have rights and the sea or a tree frog does not? If a company is harmed, that company can represent itself and stand up for its rights in court. No one is surprised by that these days. So why should a tree frog not also claim its rights? Or, as I mentioned above, what about the rights of an ocean or a river? If you think about it, surely it cannot be right that a company, which is a non-living thing, can be treated as a person under the law but a living animal or natural area cannot? In this sense, the question of the 82 trees is very relevant. It says something about who we are and how we (want to) relate to nature.

Our thinking about what constitutes a legal entity has a historical basis, associated with the predominant faith. Western civilisation has been influenced by the Genesis story in the Bible in which man is exhorted to subdue nature. In the Christian tradition, nature is subordinate to man. Nature and animals are approached as things, objects, and property that can be used and exploited at will for the benefit of man. Nature is almost always someone's property under the law and not autonomous; its importance is considered only indirectly at best. If you violate current nature-related laws or regulations, you may be fined, but reparation of damage caused is rarely part of the judgement; judgements are rarely remedial. In practice, nature almost always loses out to human interests and the habitats and the species of plants and animals living in them are curtailed or reduced. After many decades of the destruction of nature we are finally beginning to learn that this way of working and thinking is no longer tenable.

How can this negative trend be broken? Europe is currently working on a new regulation, the EU *Nature Restoration Law*. The EU aims to reverse the constant deterioration of nature by 2030. The new regulation should help nature to thrive and become more resilient. It will increase the capacity for CO2 storage to protect us from the effects of climate change. This will help EU member states to meet their climate goals of restoring 30% of their degraded ecosystems by 2030, 90% by 2050. Cities will have to be greener; rivers will have to flow freely again; farmers will have to strengthen biodiversity and forests will have to be managed more naturally. There are other fantastic developments around the world where nature is regaining its rights. This deserves a closer look:

Ecuador's conservation and restoration of ecosystems, biodiversity and genetic wealth are of public interest, according to Ecuadorian legislators and judges. Nature has even had 'constitutional' status since 2008. Under the Ecuadorian constitution, any person can now file a lawsuit in the name of nature to safeguard its rights. Thus, lawsuits have been heard concerning the Vilcabamba River, mining activities in biodiversity hotspots and shark finning. More than half of the nature rights lawsuits in Ecuador have been won.

The rights of the severely polluted Atrato River in Colombia were recognised in 2016. Local communities, represented by, among others the Centro de Estudios para la Justicia Social Tierra Digna, were vindicated by Colombia's constitutional court when they requested an *acción de tutela*, i.e., an action to protect the fundamental rights to life, health, water, food security, a healthy environment, and the culture and territory of local ethnic communities. The court also recognised the rights of the Atrato River as an autonomous entity with its own rights. Colombian judges then also declared national parks, several rivers, Lake Tota, the Colombian Amazon Forest and animals as subjects of law.

These developments are not limited to Central and South America. New Zealand has also taken action to establish laws to protect nature that are based on centuries-old traditions. Like many other indigenous peoples, New Zealand's Māori people have a culturally distinct understanding of ecological wellbeing, wherein humans are related to the sea, the wind and the forest. They put nature and its intrinsic value first, divorced from human interests. After a long struggle by the Māoris, New Zealand recognised the Whanganui River as a 'living entity with rights' in 2017. The law now literally says: 'I am the river – the river is me'. The river stands on its own; it is neither property nor a saleable object. With this recognition, the Whanganui River can now be legally represented by a body that includes guardians – people from the government and the Māori community – who, like for corporations, can stand up for the intrinsic values of the river. In Bangladesh too, all rivers have been recognised as living beings with legal status and, meanwhile, more than 20 countries have officially recognised the rights of rivers, forests, lakes, animals or even glaciers and waterfalls.

As our cultures mix, hybridise and merge, attitudes are also mixing, and we are reaching new understandings – think also of the rise of the UBUNTU philosophy ('I am because we are') (a charitable group focused on Africa) – in which intrinsic value is regaining its place and where giving rights to nature can help prevent the further degradation of natural ecosystems. The advantage of giving rights to nature is that it becomes less dependent on non-specific rules and laws. In the current situation, it is often impossible to stand up for nature if direct involvement cannot be demonstrated. The 82 trees would qualify to become co-plaintiffs in the climate case, if they were granted a legal 'personality' under the law, because their right to healthy tree life would be violated.

Like the 82 trees in Belgium, nature's rights have been attracting attention for some time now and are being raised at the highest global level, both at the International Union for the Conservation of Nature (IUCN), the world's largest nature umbrella organisation, and at the United Nations. Meanwhile, in the European Union too, people are examining nature's rights within EU law. In the Netherlands, there are calls for the creation of a new public-law legal entity, the *natuurschap*, and debates are being organised to give legal personality to the North Sea. Last year, the Frisian municipality of Noardeast-Fryslân passed a motion to grant rights to the Wadden Sea, and there are initiatives too in the UK. Recently – in April 2022 – a petition to give rights to nature also reached the European continent. 'Mar Menor', a saltwater lagoon on the Mediterranean coast near Murcia is the largest seawater lake located in Spain. The saltwater lake and its entire catchment area is the first natural ecosystem to acquire its own legal personality in Europe.

The assignation of rights to nature is not only a hot topic of discussion between scientists and lawyers worldwide, but it is also becoming common practice. Granting rights to nature represents a paradigm shift in the philosophical approach to nature in the West. It is unclear if this shift will help to solve the many shortcomings of 'modern' environmental legal perspectives, laws, directives and regulations. But it is an interesting development that is being taken very seriously in academia. National and international legislation on behalf of the rights of nature is no longer imaginary. Meanwhile, existing environmental law is also moving towards the recognition of the intrinsic value of nature to give it primacy over property rights. These laws include the imposition of remedial measures for ecological damage. Increasingly they give environmental and nature organisations wide access to courts. In any case, these developments are very promising. We can be somewhat reassured that initiatives are being taken all over the world to save nature from further destruction with growing support from the law. Perhaps we should dare to be a little more ambitious in this respect.

The Universal Rights of Nature

The UN Declaration of Human Dependence on Nature

Nature is now walking the same path as we humans have walked to gain rights. We sometimes forget that human rights did not come about by themselves either and that we had to draw them up and ratify them ourselves. This required international agreements at the very highest levels. Moreover, violation of human rights only receives widespread or international attention when people are grossly abused, and millions of victims are killed. The battles for human rights have been hard fought and laws have been slow to follow and implement. For instance, there have been several instances of genocide in non-western countries that received no international sanction nor were actions taken to defend victims. An example from my own country, Belgium, was the Congolese genocide of 8-10 million people with millions of people seriously injured (1880-1910).

The genocide that took place during World War II led to the realisation that human rights needed to be addressed in the international context. International human rights legislation resulted from initiatives that were hard fought by the world community after World War II. The result was legislation and the creation of institutions where we ordinary citizens could seek justice.

Several new legal institutions were required to support these developments. In 1945, the United Nations (UN) was established as the successor to the League of Nations with the main goal of preventing wars in the future and safeguarding world peace. It was at this time that human rights, international law, global security, development of the world economy and scientific research into social and cultural developments entered the international agenda. Currently, almost every recognised country – now totalling 193 – has joined the United Nations as a member state. This makes the UN the most important global policy organisation having the authority to make binding agreements for its member states. However obvious making agreements between all countries in the world may seem, it only became a reality with the creation of the UN.

One of the UN's most striking and significant achievements was the adoption of the *Universal Declaration of Human Rights* (UDHR) at the United Nations General Assembly on 10 December 1948. For the first time in history, human rights were recognised internationally; a unique event. Thirty different articles described the basic rights – fundamental rights – of human beings. Then, in 1950, the *European Convention on Human Rights and Fundamental Freedoms* (ECHR) was signed. Both conventions have become of great significance as a general moral standard and legal basis; they are frequently used as sources for new international treaties, they are referenced in national constitutions, and they form a basis for the work of human rights activists and organisations. As normal as it may seem today, it is only with these treaties that we global citizens have gained rights that we can claim in court. These rights include things like the right to live freely, equally and in fraternity with each other (Article 1 UDHR), the right to claim all rights and freedoms without distinction of race, colour, sex and origin (Article 2 UDHR) and the right to claim your rights to life, liberty and inviolability (Article 3 UDHR).

Nature faces the danger of extermination. Now it is nature's turn to claim its rights too. It is now time for the global community to recognise that we are inextricably linked to and dependent on biodiversity and natural ecosystems, that nature sustains humanity and not the other way around, and that nature can save humanity. With the mass extinction of species of plants and animals, the destruction of biodiversity and dangerous climate change, the world is currently undergoing a similar, possibly worse, tragedy than we faced during World War II; a tragedy that permeates the deepest fibres of the planet and society. We are faced with the greatest challenge ever; we are challenged to prevent the collapse of our planet. We are at the highest alert stage ever and it is truly high time for the world community to recognise this, to speak out and to unite in this global planetary emergency. The entire global community – everyone and everything – will have to make additional efforts to meet this challenge. It is of critical importance that the highest policy body – the United Nations – sets a strong example.

International organisations have begun to take the rights of nature seriously and it has also become a theme in academic discourse. In 2017, for instance, the EUROPARC Conference held at the Montanhas Mágicas in Portugal was organised around the theme *New Voices, New Visions, New Values – for People and Nature in Europe*. Since its foundation in 1973 in Basel, Switzerland, and after more than 40 years of successful operation, it was time to demonstrate that international nature organisations do not belong on the sidelines, but at the centre of international decision making. During the conference, elections for the council (board of directors) also took place. I ran for the presidency for a second and last time. Together with my colleagues on the council and director Carol Ritchie, we organised our annual international conference at a very high level. It was attended by influential people, including EU Commissioner Karmenu Vella and Humberto Delgado Rosa, Director for Natural Capital at the European Commission, Erika Stanciu, former State Secretary of Romania, and Dominique Leveque, Mayor of Aÿ-Champagne in France. I had also managed to persuade Monsignor Francisco Froján Madero of the Secretariat of State of the Holy See, who works most closely with the Pope, and Marina Silva, Brazil's former environment minister to attend. As icing on the cake, António Guterres, Secretary-General of the United Nations, gave a video address. The conference came at the right time. After the Paris Climate Agreement in 2015, Europe began to reflect on its position on climate and nature in global politics. Pope Francis had also received strong support from nature organisations in the same year and set out the church's position on nature, climate and sustainability in his encyclical *Laudato Si*, and the first voices were raised to declare a planetary emergency at the United Nations.

Over the past few years, the Earthshot concept has evolved into a kick-off point in my mind: a catalyst to be activated in the future when we declare our dependence on nature, when we finally realise that it is not us who will save the tree frog, it is the tree frog that will save us.

So, in 2017 at the EUROPARC conference, I was ready, confident and focused to deliver a firm global message to the international audience and to our network. It was time to make a clear statement on the international stage, time to express my seriousness. My message was: 'We depend on nature and saving nature is saving ourselves. If world peace can be guarded by UN Blue Helmets, then the nature of our planet can be protected by UN Green Helmets.' The big word was out. It was time to take action.

One first and very important outcome was the adoption of resolution 73/600 by the United Nations General Assembly on 28 July 2022, making a healthy and clean environment a human right ('the human right to a clean, healthy and sustainable environment'). The resolution calls on states, international organisations and companies to step up their efforts for a healthy environment for all. This resolution has no direct impact nor is it legally binding, but morally it is hugely important because it can, for example, encourage certain member states to introduce stricter environmental laws. Lawyers involved in climate disputes say the resolution can help them build arguments in cases where the environment and human rights are at risk.

UN Secretary-General António Guterres welcomed the 'historic' decision, saying that this landmark development shows that member states can work together in the collective fight against the triple planetary crisis of climate change, biodiversity loss and pollution. This resolution can help reduce environmental injustices, close protection gaps and empower people, especially those in vulnerable situations, such as human rights defenders, children, youth, women and indigenous peoples. A healthy environment as a human right is a major international boost and makes room for a necessary and new separate universal declaration that establishes and secures human dependence and connection with nature once and for all.

'If the bee disappeared from the globe, humans would only have four years to live. No more bees, no more pollination, no more plants and no more animals, no more humans.' There are different opinions on to whom this quote may be attributed. Many think it was Albert Einstein. Whoever it was, it is the perfect representation of what is going on: when nature disappears, humans will eventually disappear too. We depend on nature. Nature can do perfectly well without us; we, however, cannot do without nature. So, I ask the obvious question: if nature is vital, existential, for the survival of mankind, should we not only voice our 'dependence' on nature but also officially establish it as the guiding principle of life?

A beautiful idea can be put into words and words can produce legislation that can be enacted. What can be done for a citizen can also be done for nature, upon which we are so dependent. We can take inspiration from Eleanor Roosevelt, former First Lady of the US and wife of President Franklin D. Roosevelt. She delivered an historic speech in 1958 on the tenth anniversary of the Universal Declaration of Human Rights, saying: 'Where do universal human rights begin? In small places, close to home – so close and so small that they cannot be seen on any map of the world. But those places are the world of individual people; the neighbourhood he lives in; the school he attends; the factory, farm or offices where he works. If these rights have no meaning there, they have little meaning anywhere else.' Suppose we were to make the same speech today, but the topic was nature? A statement like Eleanor Roosevelt's could provide a similar general moral standard and legal basis for member states and provide additional support for the work of nature and other organisations seeking to stop the destruction of biodiversity.

> If nature is vital, existential, for the survival of mankind, should we not only voice our 'dependence' on nature but also officially establish it as the guiding principle?

I am not a lawyer, but I advocate an official declaration of our dependence on nature. The Universal Declaration of Human Dependence on Nature (UDHDN) as a new, powerful and distinct UN declaration that would describe and establish our dependence on nature. It would be ratified by the member states of the United Nations and – like the Universal Declaration of Human Rights (UDHR) – it would incorporate the rights of nature. Analysis of the UDHR shows that its knock-on effects and impact have been large and its time horizon permanent. And what are the minimum elements that a Universal Declaration on Nature should contain? Finessing the legal terminology is obviously a role for lawyers, but I call on everyone to discuss and improve the wording and, above all, to support the demand for the Universal Declaration of Human Dependence on Nature and help submit the draft declaration to the United Nations General Assembly.

Universal Declaration of Human Dependence on Nature (UDHDN)

Observing that the referral term 'nature' comprises the sum total of any living organisms, their territories, the ecosystems they are a part of, and any hereto connected self-sustaining ecological processes;

Observing that human dependence of nature should be protected by the rule of law;

Observing that it is of the greatest importance that the concept of human dependence on nature be acknowledged, agreed upon and promoted among and between nations;

Observing that Member States have pledged themselves to achieve, in cooperation with the United Nations, the promotion of universal respect for and observance of human dependence of nature;

Observing that a common understanding of human dependence on nature is of the greatest importance for the full realization of this pledge;

Now, therefore,

The General Assembly of the United Nations

should proclaim

this Universal Declaration of Dependence on Nature

as a common standard of achievement for all peoples and all nations, to the end that every individual and every organ of society, keeping this Declaration constantly in mind, shall strive by teaching and education to promote respect for these rights and freedoms and by progressive measures, national and international, to secure their universal and effective recognition and observance, both among the peoples of Member States of the United Nations themselves and among the peoples of territories under their jurisdiction:

Article 1: All human beings share a human inseparable dependence on nature;
Article 2: Nature has an intrinsic and inalienable right to be;
Article 3: Nature has the right to be protected and to protect any and all life forms and their territories, great or small, close by and far away, at this point and at any point in the future;
Article 4: Nature has the right to be restored, developed, safeguarded and maintained into self-regulating ecosystems;
Article 5: Nature is the basis for all human development;
Article 6: All human beings have the right of access to nature and a healthy environment.

From UN *Blue Helmets to* UN *Green Helmets*

A question inherent to obtaining rights is, of course, to what extent the rights can be enforced. The promotion, observation and monitoring of the UDHDN and prevention of their violation will require funding and other resources from the UN.

The UN Blue Helmets, the peacekeeping force of the UN, form an army with ample experience in the protection and enforcement of rights – sometimes more and sometimes less successfully. Their remit is to guard the security and stability of world peace. They are dispatched by the UN Security Council when international conflict threatens to break out. Their task is mainly to monitor a possible ceasefire and mediate or disarm troops as a sincere effort by the world to protect human rights. The United Nations is committed to pursuing international peace and security, developing friendly relations between nations and promoting cooperation to solve international problems.

But what about the rights of nature? An internationally accepted mechanism that can intervene both legally and physically in the event of an imminent emergency is needed to stop biodiversity loss and to restore and manage natural ecosystems. Small and large (international) organisations and partnerships have already been created for this purpose. For instance, as president of EUROPARC Federation for seven years (2014-2021), I led the largest network organisation for protected natural areas and natural heritage in Europe. With more than 400 members in 40 European countries, we manage some 40 million hectares of protected natural areas, about half of Europe's Natura 2000. Together with many other organisations and public bodies, we are trying, standing shoulder to shoulder, to restore and protect nature and take initiatives to halt the decline of biodiversity.

Amazing and selfless work is already being done by organisations, agencies and companies and by the many volunteers and individuals, young people, politicians and business leaders. Without them, the situation would be much more pronounced. Unfortunately, all this is not enough. Nature and biodiversity continue to deteriorate. Moreover, protecting nature is not always a peaceful activity as we in the West may imagine. Park Rangers risk their lives every day to protect wildlife and parkland from poaching and other threats. It is estimated that more than 1,000 Park Rangers have been killed in the last decade in the line of duty. Many of these rangers were killed by commercial poachers and armed militias. Park Rangers are generally ill-equipped, underpaid, and often undervalued.

Therefore, with the stability of our planet in jeopardy and calls for a planetary emergency, it makes sense to extend the force and create 'UN Green Helmets' alongside the UN Blue Helmets. This new force would monitor and restore biodiversity and nature around the world and fight climate change. UN Green Helmets would be deployed as an additional and complementary nature-protection force when ecosystems are being threatened and practices are being used that are in violation of climate protection legislation. The UN Green Helmets could help the already hard-working and existing organisations and agencies

The first question asked on the proposal for the UN Green Helmets could be if it is too idealistic, or even if it is feasible. That is the wrong question. The right question should be whether it is necessary.

in greening and thus cooling our planet. They could help plant the necessary billions of trees in the rainforest and equatorial forest, prevent ivory poaching, restore marshes, revitalise marine wildlife, build major water projects, carry out major reintroductions of species, stop pollution and so forth.

I expect to be asked if my proposal to ratify the UDHDN and to establish The UN Green Helmets is too *idealistic*, or even if it is *feasible*. My answer would be that the question itself is the wrong one. The right question would: Is there a need for all of this? Is declaring our dependence on nature and establishing an enforcement force *necessary*?

If you are dying and you still have some chance of survival, you do not ask questions about feasibility, you want to recover as soon as possible, whatever the cost. Saving our ailing planet and ourselves is not a question of feasibility, it is a necessity. We must save nature. We must protect the climate. We must provide the means to make the rescue operation possible. Exactly as we did to combat the coronavirus pandemic.

I can reassure those who doubt the feasibility of my proposal with facts and figures. But first, I must point out that we have no choice but to make the plan feasible because the cost of doing nothing or too little will be many times higher. A recent report (2019) by the Organisation for Economic Co-operation and Development (OECD), reviewed the financial impact of the ongoing damage to the environment. Globally, the services provided to us by nature (ecosystem services) represent an estimated USD 125-140 trillion a year, which is one and a half times the size of global GDP. The cost of inaction on biodiversity loss is immense. Between 1997 and 2011, the world lost an estimated USD 10-32 trillion a year in ecosystem services due to changing land use and land degradation. As biodiversity protection is fundamental to achieving food security, poverty reduction and a more inclusive and equitable society, the report calls for urgent action to halt and restore biodiversity and ecosystem loss. What do the UN Blue Helmets cost? The approved budget for the operation of the 70,000 UN Blue Helmets (1 July 2020-30 June 2021) is USD 6.58 billion. One could assume a similar cost for UN Green Helmets.

A simple calculation makes it clear that setting up the UN Green Helmets would be far less expensive than the cost of not having them in place, plus the force could offer employment for tens of thousands of people living in places where the demand for additional jobs and the need for biodiversity restoration are high.

Hope – how can you contribute

Something else special happened in the 'slipstream' of the EUROPARC conference in Portugal, something that still moves me deeply when I reflect on it. Marina Silva, Brazil's former environment minister, asked if she could speak to me on the evening of my arrival. I had known Marina for some time as she is a fellow recipient of the Goldman Environmental Prize, and I supported her in her fight against deforestation at the Earth Summit in Rio de Janeiro in 2012. When we met that evening she said, 'My friend, I would like your advice on whether I should run for president of Brazil again.' Marina Silva, the Amazonian girl with a dream to protect the rainforest who went on to become a nature activist and environment minister of one of the largest countries in the world, asked me for this advice? I had goose bumps when I responded, 'Yes, please do'. Marina ran for president, but she did not win. Yet I will never forget that magical moment in Portugal. However, something magical happened eventually. The former president, Lula da Silva, won the 2022 presidential election and without hesitation he reinstated Marina Silva as environment minister. As a girl of the Amazon Forest, Silva knows that action must be taken quickly. In June 2023, she and President Lula da Silva established the plan to protect 'the lungs of the earth' and stop deforestation in the Amazon Forest by 2030. Tears flowed down my cheeks when I learned the news. I was intensely happy and messaged her: 'Never give up'.

The world is changing fast. On 23 March 2021, the ship 'Evergreen' ran aground in the Suez Canal in Egypt. A single ship stuck for six days in the canal caused global disruption in the supply of goods and cost USD 9.6 billion per day due to trade disruption. On 24 February 2022, Russia attacked Ukraine. Are we heading for outright collapse on all fronts? Is there any hope?

I was elected president of the Bond Beter Leefmilieu (BBL) in June 2022, the largest umbrella organisation for nature and the environment in Flanders. It is time for a new chapter of connection and rapid transition to a nature-rich, renewable, regenerative society? War and energy crises dominate the world press and the symptoms of planetary collapse remain, yet I am still full of renewable energy. I am confident and I remain hopeful.

Hope is not the condition of waiting for things to get better. On the contrary. On her request, I presented *An Evening with Jane Goodall* in Brussels on 2 December 2022. Dr Jane Goodall, the world-renowned ethologist (behavioural biologist) and conservationist, first set foot in what is now Gombe National Park in Tanzania more than 60 years ago to begin her pioneering chimpanzee behavioural studies. Over the last six decades, this research has changed the scientific perception of the relationship between humans and the rest of the animal kingdom. Today, Jane's mission has grown into a quest to empower every individual to make the world a better place for humans, other animals and the planet we share.

It was a special evening that I will never forget. One thousand two hundred people, including hundreds of young people, listened passionately to Jane's words, just as I did. Jane's talk met with enormous enthusiasm that increased even more when she spoke about hope. She said: 'Yes, there is hope. Active hope, where we must roll up our sleeves to make it happen.' Wow, is it that simple? I was struck by Jane's perspective, one that is shared by Greta Thunberg: 'When we start to act, hope is everywhere. So instead of looking for hope, look for action. Then hope will come.' So, hope is not sitting still or waiting. Hope is the exact opposite. Hope is action, hope is doing.

Just before the conclusion of an already memorable evening, Jane Goodall looked me in the eyes and without saying a single word she gave me the same message the tree frog gave me 30 years ago: to save nature is to save ourselves.

An emotional moment with Jane Goodall: 'Saving nature is saving ourselves'.
(PHOTO CREDIT: Uli Schillebeeckx)

Working towards a world where biodiversity has returned, where our climate is protected and where industry and agriculture, governments and citizens, conservationists and entrepreneurs have joined forces, seems like the description of a utopian world. Yet there are plenty of examples of world leaders and citizens working together and setting huge movements in motion. They just did it. We must remember that in nature we have a faithful ally and a survivor.

Nature has a resilience that amazes me as a conservationist time and again. I can list many examples of it. In 2011, for example, 20 years after I came face to face with the tree frog, the popular TV programme *Animals in Nests* (*Dieren in Nesten*, in Dutch) went in search of the lynx in Belgium. There were increasing indications that this species that had vanished from Belgium had returned, and the programme's producers were keen to contribute to the research. A team of experts worked with biologists and lynx experts and the Hoge Kempen National Park rangers were deployed to find a lynx. I was hiking in the High Fens in the Ardennes with Lara Klaassen, director of the Centre for Environment and Nature Education in Maastricht, in preparation for 'Operation Lynx'. We were among the few people at the time who had seen a lynx in the flesh in Belgium; Lara in the High Fens and me on the border with Limburg. Camera 'traps' had been installed in locations chosen with support from experts, to capture photos of any lynx that might appear. Months passed without a sign of a lynx. The disappointment turned into euphoria at the very last moment due to a totally unexpected encounter: out of nowhere, not a lynx but a wolf was captured on camera in southern Belgium. After the presumably last 'Belgian' wolf was shot in 1898, this spectacular species showed itself again for the first time. Seven years later, in 2018, wolf Naya walked into Flemish Limburg from Mecklenburg-Vorpommern, Germany. With the first cubs a year later, the establishment of wolves in Belgium was a fact.

The lynx is more devious. A first recorded image followed only in 2020 from the valley of the Semois River. The images confirmed our earlier sightings that the lynx too was indeed present in Belgium. The contribution of popular TV programmes about biodiversity helped to boost our human connection with nature. But do the wolf and the lynx also herald a new era where the rights of nature become self-evident? Do they symbolise the advent of a new policy that restores the pitiful state of the patchwork of the last scraps of nature and string them together into robust and healthy natural ecosystems? 'If you always do what you have always done, you will always get what you got,' said Henry Ford, the man who managed to make the automobile accessible to all. If we do what we have always done, we will get what we have always had, even when it comes to nature. Things urgently need to change now. Know that the state of nature would be much worse if there were no organisations and people who famously contribute to nature conservation around the world every day. People who sometimes persevere at the risk of their own lives. Every contribution matters: from a small forest or grassland to a huge jungle. All these conservationists have my heart.

With that I have come to the conclusion of this book. Occasionally, a personal contribution can grow into a standard and literally make a world of difference. And it becomes even more formidable when it turns out that a Belgian played the leading role in this. Beginning in

1865, Turnhout-born Belgian Jesuit, Father Francis Xavier Kuppens (1838-1916) spent time at the old Saint Peter's Mission on the Missouri River in the US. He travelled with the Piegan Indians, who talked passionately as they relaxed in the evening about the spectacular wilderness in the somewhat distant 'wonderland'. Father Kuppens had a chance to visit this wonderland during a bison hunt with a group of Indians in the spring of 1866. It was the region we now know as Yellowstone. Kuppens was so captivated by the extraordinary beauty of this wilderness that he decided to take action. In the spring of 1867, Kuppens's mission was visited by an official delegation led by deputy governor for the territory, General Thomas Francis Meagher. By chance a heavy snowstorm forced the delegation to extend their visit by several days. Kuppens used this opportunity to bring the natural wonders of Yellowstone to the governor's attention. Irish war hero Meagher was an influential and sensitive man and argued that if the beauty of Yellowstone was as overwhelming as Father Kuppens and the Indians had described, it should be set aside as a 'national park'.

Father Kuppens moved north to reside in Helena, the capital of the state of Montana, in 1868. Meagher became a regular visitor keen to talk about wonderland Yellowstone, each time with different delegations of scientists and politicians in tow. Finally, just before his death, the general visited Yellowstone with a large delegation. On his return, he told Father Kuppens that the visit had exceeded his expectations and that he was delighted at seeing so much grandeur and beauty. He assured Kuppens that he would make 'every effort' to give Yellowstone official conservation status.

Meagher made good on his promise. On 1 March 1872, President Ulysses S. Grant ratified the *Yellowstone Park Protection Act* establishing Yellowstone Park as the world's first national park. In 1903, the next US president Theodore Roosevelt laid the cornerstone of Roosevelt Arch at the north entrance to Yellowstone Park. On the top of the arch is a quote from the 1872 Act, the law that established Yellowstone: 'For the benefit and enjoyment of the people.' The president wanted to make it clear that if we protect nature, we get a lot in return. Now we know we can add the words 'and the protection and survival of the people': because we can only survive by protecting nature.

Sweden quickly followed suit with the designation of nine national parks in 1909, the first in Europe. The Veluwezoom National Park was established in 1930 as the first of the now total of 21 national parks in the Netherlands. It was not until 2006 that Belgium established its first park, Hoge Kempen National Park. Recently (2021) a decision was finally taken to establish about five new national parks in Belgium in the coming years.

Yet Belgium was already active in those early days of national park development. Few know that Belgium established its first national park in the Belgian Congo in 1925. In fact, the Albert National Park – named after King Albert I – was the first national park in all of Africa. Upon independence in 1969, the park was renamed Virunga National Park. The vast Virunga Park (7,769 km²) is in the eastern Democratic Republic of Congo and known worldwide for its mountain gorillas and has become one of the world's most iconic national parks.

The International Union for the Conservation of Nature (IUCN), the largest network for protected natural areas in the world, published a classification method for protected natural areas in 1969. The IUCN advocated management objectives that included minimum objectives for national parks. This classification method is recognised by inter-national bodies such as the United Nations and by many national governments as the global standard for defining and registering protected areas, and as such is increasingly being incorporated into government legislation. There are now some 4,000 national parks on our planet – more than 500 of those in Europe – with enormous biodiversity that new areas can be connected to.

National parks are often the biodiversity hotspots where the fan-tastic BBC nature series with David Attenborough are filmed. They are vital for many species of plants and animals that spend their entire lives there, but sometimes only act as temporary quarters for breeding, over-summering, wintering or resting. Quite a few animals migrate over long distances, even between continents. The protection of the nightjar or the black stork, for example, depends on the opportunities and space they get in their breeding areas in Europe, on the perma-nence and quality of migration links, as well as on their wintering sites in Africa. Hence, each region also bears great responsibility for the survival and conservation of migratory species and the restoration and protection of their habitats. But above all, national parks and other protected natural areas are often the last places where species can survive. They act as a kind of waiting room from which species of plants and animals can eventually move to occupy new habitats.

Our neoliberal lifestyle has turned large parts of the world into an ecological desert. Although there is little left of our nature in some places, we cannot expect Africa or South America to take over this responsibility forecast. We have no right to ask others to protect the Amazon Forest if we have not yet managed to get our own backyard in order. This would reflect a very narrow and degrading view. The western world has a crushing responsibility.

Belgian Father Kuppens deserves a place on the list of the world's heroes. His passion and perseverance convinced the government to dedicate land as the first national park in the us and worldwide, leading eventually to the building of a system of national parks around the world. Fortunately, the time of religious conversions in which Kuppens operated are over. We now appreciate that local, indigenous population groups are much better able to both protect nature and take responsibility for it. They deserve every support – including financial support – to restore and protect nature, and with it, to protect the bridge to a biodiverse and sustainable planet.

I am often asked: 'What can I do myself? Can I contribute as an individual to help prevent the destruction of the planet?' You absolutely can. You can eat more consciously, move more consciously, create or join a nature association, roll up your sleeves and build a natural garden or nature terrace, become politically active, donate money to charities, and so on. There are great websites that will calculate your carbon footprint and give tips on how to live more nature-friendly, sustainable, climate-conscious and socially responsible lives. Do not hold yourself back from looking. Keep yourself informed and talk about it. And as a golden tip: take a moment every day to reflect on your own actions and how you can improve them. Dare to look in the mirror and

Nature does not send a bill,
it is not asking for money.
Nature is asking for her rights.
All nature wants is to exist;
nature just wants to be.

ask yourself what bees get in return for pollinating blossoms, marshes for purifying water, forests and seas for purifying and cooling the air. Recognise the interdependencies of life.

Nature never charges for its beauty and the services it provides to us. Even if you don't love nature, you get to enjoy it for free. We have taken and still take it for granted and we have forgotten and still forget to give value to it. How long will we remain blind to our existential connection and deaf to nature's alarm signals? With rapidly increasing occurrences of heat waves, floods and hurricanes, the impact of viral pandemics and the loss of species and habitats, we are now confronted daily with nature's bill. But nature is not asking for money. Nature is asking for her rights. All nature wants is to exist; nature just wants to be. Now that we realise that nature is our only real lifeline, we must restore and protect her so that she can keep us alive. Financing the repair of the destruction we caused is therefore not a cost, but an investment in our own protection.

At the beginning of this book, I wrote: 'I am because we are.' We must realise and acknowledge that people cannot survive without nature, nor without each other. In a society, no single individual can do everything, there is no 'them' nor 'us', there is only 'together'. A community, a society is essentially 'living together'. There is a role for everyone in a society. The time has come to break down the walls that separate us, to restore our connections and to invest in a sustainable future. Above all, investing also means planting trees under which we ourselves will never sit, restoring the climate for our children and grandchildren. Chief Seattle, head of the Suquamish and Duwamish tribes in Washington state, once said: 'We do not inherit the earth from our ancestors, we borrow it from our children.'

This is the power of the (Re)connection Model: genuinely reconnecting with one another as a society in the wake of nature where everyone is responsible and contributes to the restoration and conservation of biodiversity and natural ecosystems: where we decide together that we cannot destroy what keeps us alive. We are ready to design new regulatory frameworks for the rights of nature; this framework together with a Universal Declaration of Human Dependence on Nature are the foundations for and keys to the future. Let us not destroy what keeps us alive. We are nature. It is time for biodiversity.

"Something is nothing
until nothing is something."

Meanwhile, 30 years have passed since the tree frog had a message for me. The message was that we cannot live without each other; that if we manage to save nature, nature will protect us. I am not blind to the ongoing destruction of nature, nor deaf to the disbelief of those who think everything will work itself out. Out of love for the planet, I stand up for the climate and the rights of nature and I call for the Universal Declaration of Human Dependence on Nature to be debated and ratified.

I have witnessed the overwhelming beauty and resilience of nature in all its manifestations in my search for answers and explanations. I learned that what we dare not dream will never become reality. I have dreamed of untamed challenges in the wilderness. Dreams became thoughts and thoughts became words. More than once I have been in fear of failure or loss, but my belief in the possibility of victory was always greater than my fear.

My dreams became reality in the first place thanks to the team of the Regional Landscape Kempen and Maasland (RLKM), the best team in the world. I learned that a strong partnership in a small region in a small country can write a big story, that local solutions can form bridges to meet global challenges.

Big thanks to the boards of RLKM, all partners and stakeholders – local and international – for their support and faith. Thank you municipalities, province of Limburg and Flanders.

The Goldman Environmental Prize, Ashoka and EUROPARC Federation gave me the wings I so desperately wanted to fly with. Together we fly to and colour the rainbow. I learnt to listen to the call of the tree frog and increasingly recognise the heartbeat of nature. I learned how to translate nature to give it a louder and stronger voice. I learned how to amplify nature's value and share.

Time and again I have had unexpected encounters in nature; time and again I have looked with pride to the clever achievements of many passionate and inspiring colleagues, friends, people and organisations. I am immensely grateful for the many acknowledgements I have received but know that they also belong to all of you. What I have learned above all is that no one can do everything, and everyone can do something. And that together is much more than a mere summation of parts; that the whole is much more than the sum of its parts.

If we save nature, nature will protect us.

Many thanks to everyone from far and near who supported and participated in this book. If you are one of them: sincere thanks. Thank you to Rein and Dominic. Thank you to Jan Colruyt for supporting the English translation.

And an especially sincere word of thanks to my wife Carine and daughter Merle. Without you this would never have been possible.

Think globally, act locally and change personally!

Getting to work

Nature

- *The UN Convention on Biological Diversity*:
  https://www.cbd.int/

- *The Global Diversity Outlook* (fifth edition):
  https://www.cbd.int/gbo5

- European Environmental Agency:
  https://www.eea.europa.eu/nl

- *State of Nature in the EU*, the latest report from that European
  Environmental Agency:
  https://www.eea.europa.eu/publications/state-of-nature-in-the-eu-2020

- *A comprehensive definition of biodiversity* in *The Stanford Encyclopaedia of Philosophy*:
  https://plato.stanford.edu/entries/biodiversity/

- More info on planetary boundaries can be found on Stockholm Resilience's
  website, under *The nine planetary boundaries*, or in the articles *Planetary Boundaries: Exploring the Safe Operating Space for Humanity* and *Planetary Boundaries: Guiding human development on a changing plane* (Steffen et al.,
  2015):
  www.stockholmresilience.org
  https://www.ecologyandsociety.org/vol14/iss2/art32/

- WWF's Living Planet Report 2020:
  https://www.wwf.nl/wat-we-doen/actueel/nieuws/
  wwf-living-planet-report-2020

- Read about ecological footprint:
  https://www.footprintnetwork.org/our-work/ecological-footprint/

- Information on the evolution of viruses (and more specifically coronavirus), read WWF's paper *Covid 19: Urgent Call to Protect People and Nature*:
  https://wwfeu.awsassets.panda.org/downloads/wwf_covid19_urgent_call_to_protect_people_and_nature_1.pdf

- To learn about the philosophy of *Lassen Natur Natur sein*, you can read BUND *Naturshutz* (in German):
  https://www.bund-naturschutz.de/ueber-uns/erfolge-niederlagen/nationalpark-bayerischer-wald/philosophie-natur-natur-sein-lassen

- You can find raw data on population growth at the website *Our World in Data*:
  https://ourworldindata.org/world-population-growth

- *The Nature Report Flanders 2020*:
  https://www.vlaanderen.be/inbo/publicaties/natuurrapport-2020-toestand-van-de-natuur-in-vlaanderen

- Info on policies concerning nature protection and biodiversity in the Netherlands can be found at the central government or *Natuurmonumenten*:
  https://www.rijksoverheid.nl/onderwerpen/natuur-en-biodlversiteit/beschermde-natuurgebieden
  https://www.rijksoverheid.nl/onderwerpen/natuur-en-biodiversiteit/bescherming-biodiversiteit-nederland
  https://www.natuurmonumenten.nl/standpunten/biodiversiteit

- The European Environment Agency has an overview of protected areas within Europe:
  https://www.eea.europa.eu/publications/protected-areas-in-europe-2012

- On midwife toads and partial albinism in Limburg:
  https://www.limburg.be/Limburg/Natuurcentrum/Natuurcentrum-Meta/Jaarboek-%20Likona/Partieel-Albinisme-bij-Vroedmeesterpadden-te-Borgloon,-Belgie.html

- The Council of Europe teaches you about the *Bern Convention*:
  https://www.coe.int/en/web/bern-convention

- At the website *Rewilding Europe*, you can find out about the return of large carnivores to Europe:
  https://rewildingeurope.com/rewilding-in-action/wildlife-comeback/large-carnivores/

- Europe's take on those large carnivores:
  https://ec.europa.eu/environment/nature/conservation/species/carnivores/faq.htm#How%%2020are%20large%20carnivores%20doing%20in%20Europe

– Knowledge about the relationship between biodiversity and protected areas can be found at *Nature's* website in the article entitled *Local Biodiversity is higher inside than outside terrestrial protected areas worldwide*:

https://www.nature.com/articles/ncomms12306#:~:text=Abstract,conside-red%20essential%2020for%20biodiversity%20conservation.&text=Global-ly%2C%20species%20richness%20is%20%2010.6,richness%20nor%20endemicity%20differ%20significantly

– Read about island theory / island biogeography by searching on the *Science Direct* and *Stanford University* websites:

https://www.sciencedirect.com/topics/earth-and-planetary-sciences/island-biogeography and https://web.stanford.edu/group/stanfordbirds/text/essays/Island_Biogeography.html#:~:tex%20t=Wilson%20of%20Harvard%2C%20developed%20a,of%20established%20species%20becom%20e%20extinct

– You can learn about ecosystem services in IPBES's *Global Assessment Report on Biodiversity and Ecosystem Services*:

https://ipbes.net/global-assessment and https://ipbes.net/news/Media-Release-Global-Assessment

– WWF's *Living Planet Index*:

https://wwf.panda.org/discover/knowledge_hub/all_publications/living_planet_index2/? https://wwf.be/assets/IMAGES-2/CAMPAGNES/LPR2020/LPR20-Full-report-LQ.pdf

– On Europe's strategy around biodiversity:

https://ec.europa.eu/info/strategy/priorities-2019-2024/european-green-deal/actions-being-taken-eu/eu-biodiversity-strategy-2030_nl https://eurlex.europa.eu/legalcontent/NL/TXT/HTML/?uri=CELEX:52020DC0380&from=EN

– On the link between the international footprint and deforestation, there is WWF's report *The Risk of Corruption and Forest Loss in Belgium's Imports of Commodities*:

https://wwf.be/nl/publicatie/risk-corruption-and-forest-loss-belgiums-imports-commodities

– On the quality of our marine nature, WWF published the article *Ocean Wealth valued at 24 trillion USD*:

https://wwf.panda.org/wwf_news/?244770/Ocean-wealth-valued-at-US24-trillion-but-sinking-fast

– You can read about the illegal animal trade in WWF's CITES report *Not for Sale - Halting the Illegal Trade of CITES Species from World Heritage Sites*:

https://files.worldwildlife.org/wwfcmsprod/files/Publication/file/5hei86izjg_CITES_FINAL_ENG.pdf

- You can read about the Sandford principle on Wikipedia:
  https://en.wikipedia.org/wiki/Sandford_Principle

- Father Kuppens's letter about the Yellowstone National Park start-up:
  https://jesuitonlinelibrary bc.edu/?a=d&d=wlet18971101-01.2.8&e=-------
  en-20--1--txt-txIN-------

- Global Outlook 5 - CBD:
  https://www.cbd.int/gbo5

- *Financing the Transition: the Costs of Avoiding Deforestation* -
  Energy Transitions Commission:
  https://www.energy-transitions.org/publications/financing-the-transition-
  etc-avoiding-deforestation/

- Single Earth:
  https://www.single.earth/blog/evolution-of-climate-david-attenborough?
  4939ba4b_page=3

- *Rapid rise in urban sprawl: Global hotspots and trends since 1990*:
  https://journals.plos.org/sustainabilitytransformation/article?id=10.1371/
  journal.pstr.0000034

Climate

- The UN provides a wealth of information on climate. These include the
  Intergovernmental Panel on Climate Change (IPCC) 2021 Climate Report, the
  United Nations Environment Program (UNEP) Emissions Gap Report 2021
  and the *Climate Change Performance Index (CCPI)*:
  https://www.ipcc.ch/report/sixth-assessment-report-working-group-i/
  https://www.unep.org/resources/emissions-gap-report-2021 and
  https://ccpi.org/

- In addition, it is also best to check out the *2015 Paris Climate Agreement* on
  the UN site:
  https://unfccc.int/process-and-meetings/the-paris-agreement/the-paris-
  agreement

- As well as the *Glasgow COP 26 agreement - 2021*:
  https://unfccc.int/sites/default/files/resource/cop26_auv_2f_cover_
  decision.pdf?fbclid=IwAR2_plIoIUFlWvcztiZ3xuuzcpfF9l1Br-w5zGvNHioe2
  QiQRTSV94ARPUA

- And the IPCC's *Fifth Assessment Report*:
  https://www.ipcc.ch/report/ar5/wg2/

– For an overview, you can also find a timeline of highlights from
the IPCC's history:
https://www.ipcc.ch/site/assets/uploads/2018/04/FS_timeline.pdf

– Advertising campaigns by the oil industry intended to cast doubt on the
link between fossil fuels and climate change in comparison to IPCC's
warnings around the tipping point in the climate have been the subject
of investigative journalism by *The Guardian*:
https://www.theguardian.com/environment/2021/nov/18/the-forgotten-
oil-ads-that-told-us-climate-change-was-nothing and
https://www.theguardian.com/environment/2021/jun/23/climate-change-
dangerous-thresholds-un-report

– On greenhouse gas emissions by sector in Belgium and the Netherlands,
visit klimaat.be or the Dutch Central Bureau of Statistics:
https://klimaat.be/in-belgie/klimaat-en-uitstoot/uitstoot-van-broeikasgassen/
uitstoot-per-sector

https://www.cbs.nl/nl-nl/dossier/dossier-broeikasgassen/hoofdcategorieen/
welke-sectoren-stoten-broeikasgassen-uit-

– About the climate case in Belgium:
https://www.klimaatzaak.eu/

– The website of Urgenda's climate case against the Dutch state:
https://www.urgenda.nl/themas/klimaat-en-energie/klimaatzaak/

– The book *Revolution with Law* (2015) by lawyer Roger Cox:
https://www.revolutiemetrecht.nl/

– Milieudefensie Nederland, that won the lawsuit against oil giant Shell
https://milieudefensie.nl/actie/klimaatzaakshell

– On global trends in climate change litigation, the London School of
Economics published the paper *Global trends in climate litigation*:
https://www.lse.ac.uk/GranthamInstitute/publication/global-trends-in-
climate-change-litigation-2019-snapshot/

– In France, there is L'Affaire du Siècle:
https://laffairedusiecle.net/qui-sommes-nous/

– On climate litigation in Germany:
https://www.bundesverfassungsgericht.de/SharedDocs/Pressemitteilungen/
EN/2021/bvg21-031.html

– On climate litigation and the ground-breaking ruling in Montana (US):
https://www.washingtonpost.com/climate-environment/2023/08/14/
youths-win-montana-climate-trial/

- zme Science published a powerful article with *What is Climate* on the definition of climate, why it is not weather, and why that distinction is important:
  https://www.zmescience.com/science/what-is-climate-043242/
- Frontiers in Marine Science published on the Antarctic ice sheet:
  https://www.frontiersin.org/articles/10.3389/fmars.2021.642040/full
- On Hasselt University's Ecotron research centre:
  https://www.uhasselt.be/Ontdek-Ecotron.html
- About the Club of Rome and the climate emergency:
  https://www.clubofrome.org/impact-hubs/climate-emergency/
- *IPCC Sixth Assessment Report*:
  https://www.ipcc.ch/assessment-report/ar6/
- Refugees - Journal of Global Health:
  https://jogh.org/2023/jogh-13-03011#:~:text=Such%20figures%20are%20expected%20to,and%20climate%20change%20%5B6%5D.
- Institute for Economics and Peace:
  https://www.economicsandpeace.org/wp-content/uploads/2020/08/GPI_2020_web.pdf
- Quantifying the human cost of global warming:
  https://www.nature.com/articles/s41893-023-01132-6
- eu Eurobarometer 98 - Winter 2022-2023:
  https://europa.eu/eurobarometer/surveys/detail/2872
- Zero net by 2050:
  https://www.iea.org/reports/net-zero-by-2050
- nasa's up-to-date direct measurements on CO_2 levels offer a sobering view on the evolution of its prevalence in our atmosphere throughout the last 200 years:
  https://climate.nasa.gov/vital-signs/carbon-dioxide/#:~:text=Since%20the%20beginning%20of%20industrial,ice%20age%2020%2C000%20years%20ago

Agriculture

- fao's report *Tackling Climate Change through Livestock* (2013) looks at the impact of livestock on climate:
  http://www.fao.org/3/i3437e/i3437e00.htm

- Figures on the composition of livestock in Belgium can be found from the Flemish government:
  https://www.vlaanderen.be/vlam/sites/default/files/publications/2020-05/veestapel%20Belgi%C3%AB%20%282010-2019%29.pdf

- Ashoka can tell you about the Bioregional Weaving Labs Collective on sustainable business and sensible agriculture:
  https://www.ashoka.org/en-nl/program/bioregional-weaving-labs-collective#:~:text=Bioregional%20Weaving%20Lab%20facilitation,initiating%20partnerships%20for%20collective%20impact

- Our World in Data report on methane emissions and meat production:
  https://ourworldindata.org/carbon-footprint-food-methane

- You can read about the particular importance of biomass in the *Proceedings of the National Academy of Sciences of the United States of America* (PNAS) report *Distribution of Biomass on Earth* 2018:
  https://www.pnas.org/content/115/25/6506

- An eye opener: the evolution in global chicken numbers from 1990 to 2020:
  https://www.statista.com/statistics/263962/number-of-chickens-worldwide-since-1990/#:~:text=The%20number%20of%20chickens%20worldwide,14.38%20billion%20chickens

- Also, not to be missed: the international ranking of meat consumption:
  https://www.statista.com/chart/3707/the-countries-that-eat-the-mostmeat/#:~:text=Which%20countries%20have%20the%20biggest,(99%20kg)%20of%20meat

- The EAT, the food system transformation platform, and its *EAT-Lancet Commission's Summary Report*:
  https://eatforum.org/eat-lancet-commission/eat-lancet-commission-summary-report/

- *Reducing meat consumption in developed and transition countries to counter climate change and biodiversity loss*, an article by Susanne Stoll-Kleeman & Uta Johanna Schmidt on global deforestation to grow animal feed:
  https://link.springer.com/article/10.1007/s10113-016-1057-5

- General information on soil biodiversity:
  https://esdac.jrc.ec.europa.eu/themes/soil-biodiversity

- A special example of biological insect control: deploying parasitic wasps instead of using insecticides:
  https://edepot.wur.nl/51347

- Slow Food, an organisation ensuring access to quality, healthy, environmentally friendly and fair food for all:
https://www.slowfood.com/about-us/our-philosophy/

- *The Organic Agriculture Report of the Research Institute of Organic Agriculture* (FiBL):
https://www.fibl.org/en/info-centre/news/
european-organic-market-grew-to-euro-45-billion-in-2019

- Must-read: FAO *on biodiversity and its role in agriculture and food supply*:
https://www.fao.org/3/CA3129EN/CA3129EN.pdf

- *Greenhouse gas emissions from agrifood systems Global, regional and country trends, 2000-2020*:
https://www.fao.org/3/cc2672en/cc2672en.pdf

- Nitrogen emissions along global livestock supply chains:
https://www.nature.com/articles/s43016-020-0113-y

- The World of Organic Agriculture 2021:
https://www.fao.org/family-farming/detail/en/c/1378841/

Health

- Read about the link between biodiversity, drugs and the future of global health in the article *Biodiversity, drug discovery, and the future of global health* found on the *Journal of Global Health* website:
https://www.ncbi.nlm.nih.gov/pmc/articles/PMC5735771/

- How natural products became new sources of drugs over the last 25 years, David Newman and Gordon Cragg examined (under the title *Natural Products as sources of new drugs over the last 25 years*):
https://pubmed.ncbi.nlm.nih.gov/17309302/

- EUROPARC's *Physical Activity Guidelines Advisory Committee Report* (2008):
https://www.europarc.org/wp-content/uploads/2018/03/Physical-Activity-Guidelines- Advisory-Committee-Report-2008.pdf

- Harvard University publication on the link between burnout and nature, in the article *Get back to nature*:
https://www.health.harvard.edu/mind-and-mood/
sour-mood-getting-you-down-get-back-to-nature

- The link between nature and reduced stress (the article *Levels of Nature and Stress Response*), and on the general impact of nature on health (the article *How does nature exposure make people healthier?*), via the National Center for Biotechnology Information:
  https://www.ncbi.nlm.nih.gov/pmc/articles/PMC5981243/
  https://www.ncbi.nlm.nih.gov/pmc/articles/PMC6104990/

- On the health benefits of nature in the city, *Nature* published the article *Health Benefits from Nature Experiences Depend on Dose* (Shanahan et al):
  https://www.nature.com/articles/srep28551

- On the axolotl, its special characteristics and its endangered status, the article *Biology's beloved amphibian is racing towards extinction* appeared in *Nature*:
  https://www.nature.com/articles/d41586-017-05921-w

- On how climate change is affecting human life and health in different ways, you can find some statistics under the theme *Public Health and Environment* on the WHO website:
  https://www.who.int/data/gho/data/themes/public-health-and-environment

- Also, WHO, through its general press service, on polluted air (found through the search term 'air pollution'):
  https://www.who.int/news-room/air-pollution

Ecosystem services

- General info on ecosystem services or global value ecosystem services can be found in the work of Robert Costanza (e.g. *The Value of the World's Ecosystem Services and Natural Capital*, available free of charge via ResearchGate):
  https://www.anu.edu.au/events/the-global-value-of-ecosystem-services
  https://www.researchgate.net/publication/229086194_The_Value_of_the_World's_Ecosystem_Services_and_Natural_Capital

- On ecosystem services in the Netherlands, Statistics Netherlands provides the necessary data (e.g., *Natural Capital Accounts Netherlands 2013-2018*):
  https://www.cbs.nl/nl-nl/longread/aanvullende-statistische-diensten/2021/natuurlijk-kapitaalrekeningen-nederland-2013-2018/6-waarde-van-het-ecosysteemkapitaal#:~:text=In%202018%20was%20the%20total,11%20ecosystem services%20869%20billion%20euros

- On the international front, check out the Commission on Ecosystem Management of the International Union for the Conservation of Nature (IUCN):
https://www.iucn.org/commissions/commission-ecosystem-management/our-work/cems-thematic-groups/ecosystem-services

- On how scientific insights around ecosystem services can become more relevant in decision making, see *Increasing decision relevance of ecosystem service science*, Lisa Mandle et al:
https://www.nature.com/articles/s41893-020-00625-y

- A handy resource for information about the number of languages on Earth:
https://www.ethnologue.com/guides/how-many-languages

- More info on peak-end theory:
https://positivepsychology.com/what-is-peak-end-theory/

Economy

- The OECD *Environmental Outlook to 2050*, a numerical analysis of the environmental outlook to 2050 and the consequences of inaction:
https://www.oecd.org/env/indicators-modelling-outlooks/oecdenvironmentaloutlookto2050theconsequencesofinaction-keyfactsandfigures.htm

- The European Commission on the EU Biodiversity Strategy to 2030:
https://eur-lex.europa.eu/resource.html?uri=cellar:a3c806a6-9ab3-11ea-9d2d-01aa75ed71a1.0001.02/DOC_1&format=PDF

- Mariana Mazzucato's Wikipedia page:
https://nl.wikipedia.org/wiki/Mariana_Mazzucato

- The Dutch Central Bureau of Statistics calculated the total value of ecosystem services in the Netherlands in the *Natural Capital Accounts Netherlands 2013-2018*:
https://www.cbs.nl/nl-nl/longread/aanvullende-statistische-diensten/2021/natuurlijk-kapitaalrekeningen-nederland-2013-2018/6-waarde-van-het-ecosysteemkapitaal

- The University of Cambridge calculated the value and benefits of visiting protected areas (worldwide) in 2015, in the article *World's protected natural areas receive eight billion visits a year*:
https://www.cam.ac.uk/research/news/worlds-protected-natural-areas-receive-eight-billion-visits-a-year

– The European Commission examined the economic benefits of the Natura 2000 network in its 2013 publication *The Economic benefits of the Natura 2000-Network*:
https://ec.europa.eu/environment/nature/natura2000/financing/docs/ENV-12-018_LR_Final1.pdf

– The Flemish Environment Society published the report *Greening the tax system in Flanders* in December 2020:
https://www.milieurapport.be/publicaties/2020/vergroening-van-het-belastingstelsel

– C2C Platform awards cradle-to-cradle certificate for products:
https://www.c2cplatform.eu/

– You can find out how a tax shelter works in the subsidiary bank of VLAIO, the contact point for entrepreneurs in Flanders:
https://www.vlaio.be/nl/subsidies-financiering/subsidiedatabank/tax-shelter-audiovisuele-werken-en-podiumkunsten
https://www.vlaio.be/nl/subsidies-financiering/subsidiedatabank/tax-shelter-voor-startende-ondernemingen

– On the websites of The Institute of International Finance (via its Taskforce on Scaling Voluntary Carbon Markets) and the International Organisation for Standardisation (via, for example, the paper *Climate change mitigation*) you can find out about the voluntary carbon market and climate change mitigation as an organisation:
https://www.iif.com/tsvcm
https://www.iso.org/files/live/sites/isoorg/files/store/en/PUB100271.pdf

– On the impact of green economy on jobs, you can contact the UN (via the blog about Sustainable Development Goals) or the International Labour Organisation (via the report *World Employment and Social Outlook 2018: Greening with jobs*):
https://www.un.org/sustainabledevelopment/blog/2019/04/green-economy-could-create-24-million-new-jobs/
https://www.ilo.org/global/publications/books/WCMS_628654/lang--en/index.htm

– Research from Wageningen University & Research (via the 'biodiversity' page on their website) shows us how biodiversity represents enormous economic value:
https://www.wur.nl/nl/Onderzoek-Resultaten/Onderzoeksinstituten/Environmental-Research/Programmas/Biodiversiteit.htm#:~:text=Biodiversity%20represents%20an%20enormous%20economic,is%20dependent%20on%20biological%20resources.

- General data on the economy of Europe in this book was derived from *Facts and figures on the economy of the European Union*:
  https://european-union.europa.eu/principles-countries-history/key-facts-and-figures/economy_nl#:~:text=The%20total%20value%20of%20all,%2C%20 16%2C4%20billion%20euros

- The importance of the climate crisis for our economy can be found in the World Economic Forum's report *Nature Risk Rising* (2020):
  https://www3.weforum.org/docs/WEF_New_Nature_Economy_Report_2020.pdf

- On *The Economics of Ecosystems and Biodiversity* (TEEB):
  http://teebweb.org/

- More info on the definition of decoupling:
  https://en.wikipedia.org/wiki/Eco-economic_decoupling

- The meaning of ecosystem accounting means as interpreted by the United Nations' *System of Environmental Economic Accounting*:
  https://seea.un.org/ecosystem-accounting

- Must-read on the role of natural capital in ecosystems is *Progress in natural capital accounting for ecosystems*, Lars Hein et al:
  https://www.science.org/doi/10.1126/science.aaz8901

- The Foundations of the Doughnut Economy:
  https://www.kateraworth.com/doughnut/

- How national park visitors generate economic impact – according to the US Department of the Interior – can be found in the press release *National Park Visitor Spending Generates Economic Impact of More Than $41 Billion*:
  https://www.doi.gov/pressreleases/ national-park-visitor-spending-generates-economic-impact-more-41-billion

- The figures on the added value of the Hoge Kempen National Park can be found on the park's website and in the publication *Hoge Kempen, high benefits* (2010): https://www.nationaalparkhogekempen.be/nl/over-ons/ hoge-kempen-hoge-baten

- You can also find the ecological results of 30 years of nature development along the Grensmaas, the lifeline of the Meuse Valley River Park, on the website riverparkmaasvallei.eu:
  https://www.rivierparkmaasvallei.eu/sites/default/files/maas_in_beeld_ brochure_08_voor_website.pdf

- More on the figures and results: the *Final report on sustainable connecting, the quality impulse for the environment in the Kempen-broek Border Park and the border region*:
  https://www.grensregio.eu/assets/files/site/downloads/Eindrapport.pdf

- About Wildlife Economy (WLE):
  https://www.efro-projecten.be/nl/zoek-een-europees-project/wle-wildlife-economy~345/

- A particularly instructive report on biodiversity, finance and the economic and business case for acting as we do in the National Park is the report *Biodiversity: Finance and the Economic and Business Case for Action,* that the OECD wrote for the G7:
  https://www.oecd.org/environment/resources/biodiversity/G7-report-Biodiversity-Finance-and-the-Economic-and-Business-Case-for-Action.pdf

- *World Employment and Social Outlook - Trends 2022:*
  https://www.ilo.org/global/research/global-reports/weso/trends2022/lang--en/index.htm

- *Global Risk Report WEF 2023:*
  https://www.weforum.org/reports/global-risks-report-2023/digest

- UNEP Beyond GDP 1:30:
  https://www.unep.org/news-and-stories/story/beyond-gdp-making-nature-count-shift-sustainability

Tourism

- Indispensable: a definition of sustainable tourism can be found on the Global Sustainable Tourism Council website:
  https://www.gstcouncil.org/what-is-sustainable-tourism/

- Reading tip: the book *Green Growth and Travelism - Letters from leaders*:
  https://www.goodfellowpublishers.com/academic-publishing.php?promoCode=&partnerID=&content=story&storyID=282

- A general estimate of tourism's carbon footprint can be found in the article *Estimation of tourism carbon footprint and carbon capacity* by Tianyue Huang and Zi Tang:
  https://academic.oup.com/ijlct/article/16/3/1040/6248119

- About Metsähallitus Parks & Wildlife Finland and sustainable tourism:
  https://www.oneplanetnetwork.org/initiative/metsahallitus-parks-wildlife-finland- sustainable-nature-tourism

- Research conducted by the University of Cambridge demonstrated that, globally, protected nature reserves are visited eight billion times a year:
  https://www.cam.ac.uk/research/news/worlds-protected-natural-areas-receive-eight-billion-visits-a-year

–   For general info on tourism and its impact on nature, you can visit National Geographic (under the heading *Tourism Gone Wrong*), the World Travel & Tourism Council (*Loss of almost US$4.5 trillion in 2020*) or ResearchGate (via the article *Nature Based Tourism, Nature Based Tourism Destinations, Attributes and Nature Based Tourists' Motivations'*, by researcher Taki Can Metin), among others:

    https://www.nationalgeographic.com/travel/article/tourism-gone-wrong
    https://wttc.org/News-Article/Global-TandT-sector-suffered-a-loss-of-almost-US4-trillion-in-2020
    https://www.researchgate.net/publication/331982531_Nature_Based_Tourism_Nature_Based_Tourism_Destinations%27_Attributes_And_Nature_Based_Tourists%27_Motivations

–   On what tourist destinations themselves undertake to keep their natural assets alive:

    https://wwf.be/nl/actualiteit/belize-verbiedt-alle-olie-activiteiten-zijn-wateren

–   You can read about the carbon footprint of ecotourism packages at Footprintnetwork.org:

    https://www.footprintnetwork.org/our-work/sustainable-tourism/

Sustainable Development Goals

–   The home page for information about the goals:

    https://sdgs.un.org/goals

–   General information on the Millennium Goals can be found on the general web pages of the UN:

    https://www.un.org/millenniumgoals/

–   You can learn about the LATTE principle in the book *Latte macchiato: trends for the next decade* by Herman Konings:

    https://lib.ugent.be/nl/catalog/rug01:001794547

–   On responsible consumption, the master's thesis *Environmentally and socially responsible consumption? A study on food sustainability discourses* by Ulrike Ehgartner:

    https://www.research.manchester.ac.uk/portal/files/144410664/thesis_with_cover_page.pdf

–   For a definition of glocalisation:

    https://en.wikipedia.org/wiki/Glocalization

- The podcast episode *Ancient wisdom for brand new times* from NRC's *Future Affairs* show, with sustainability professor Pim Martens, on indigenous peoples' view of the future:
  https://www.nrc.nl/nieuws/2021/12/09/oeroude-wijsheid-voor-gloednieuwe-tijden-a4068399

Nature's rights

- Must-read: the UN Environment programme *Making peace with nature*:
  https://www.unep.org/resources/making-peace-nature

- On the impact of nature rights on the legal system, Hendrik Schoukens wrote the article *Rights of nature as a paradigm shift: the slow crumbling of a centuries-old fault line within our legal system?* in Oikos:
  https://www.oikos.be/tijdschrift/archief/jaargang-2018/oikos-86-2-2018/1165-86-02-schoukens-rechten-van-de-natuur/file

- Columbia Climate School research on whether nature can have rights appeared under the title *The Rights of Nature - Can an Ecosystem Bear Legal Rights?*:
  https://news.climate.columbia.edu/2021/04/22/rights-of-nature-lawsuits/#:~:text=What%20are%20the%20%E2%80%9CRights%20of,or%20even%20by%20climate%20change.

- The website of Embassy of the North Sea, the organisation whose operations are based on the principle that the North Sea and marine life belong to themselves:
  https://www.ambassadevandenoordzee.nl/1784-2/

- GARN, the Global Network of organisations and individuals committed to the recognition of the Rights of Nature:
  https://www.garn.org/

- What the European Parliament itself says about nature rights in Europe is best read in the report *Can Nature Get it Right? A Study on the Rights of Nature in the European Context*:
  https://www.europarl.europa.eu/RegData/etudes/STUD/2021/689328/IPOL_STU(2021)689328_EN.pdf

- On legal criticism of recognising the rights of nature, the International Union for Conservation of Nature published the article *Rights of Nature: Why it Might Not Save the Entire World* by Dr Julien Bétaille:
  https://www.iucn.org/news/world-commission-environmental-law/201905/rights-nature-why-it-might-not-save-entire-world

- The case of the Frome, a small river in England, or how an English town joined the campaign for nature rights:
  https://www.reuters.com/article/us-climate-change-britain-river-insight-idUSKCN1VV19E

- *The Universal Declaration of Human Rights*, on which the wording of the Declaration of Dependency is based:
  https://www.un.org/en/about-us/udhr/history-of-the-declaration#:~:text=The%20Universal%20Declaration%20of%20Human,of%20the%20Second%20World%20War.&text=World%20leaders%20decided%20to%20complement,rights%20of%20every%20individual%20everywhere.
  https://www.un.org/en/about-us/universal-declaration-of-human-rights

- Inspiration on the operation and budget for the Green Helmets can of course be found from its military counterpart, the Blue Helmets:
  https://peacekeeping.un.org/en/how-we-are-funded
  https://peacekeeping.un.org/en/military

- Guidelines for applying management categories for protected areas (IUCN):
  https://portals.iucn.org/library/node/30018

- Healthy environment as UN Human Right:
  https://news.un.org/en/story/2022/07/1123482

- UN Resolution - *A Human right to a clean and healthy environment* - July 28, 2022:
  https://documents-dds-ny.un.org/doc/UNDOC/GEN/N22/442/77/PDF/N2244277.pdf?OpenElement

General links

- The Kempen and Maasland Regional Landscape:
  www.rlkm.be
  www.nationaalparkhogekempen.be
  www.rivierparkmaasvallei.eu
  https://www.kempenbroek.eu/nl

- The EUROPARC Federation:
  https://www.europarc.org/

- Ashoka, the largest social entrepreneurship organisation pursuing sustainable system change:
  www.ashoka.org

- The Goldman Environmental Prize, or the 'Green Nobel Prize':
  www.goldmanprize.org

About the Author

Ignace Schops (born 1964) is a Belgian environmentalist and a biodiversity, landscape ecology and herpetology expert. He is director of the Belgian NGO 'Regionaal Landschap Kempen en Maasland' (RLKM) and president of the 'Bond Beter Leefmilieu' (BBL) which is the largest environmental network in Belgium. He is former president of the largest European natural heritage network, EUROPARC federation (2014 – 2021), and a full member of the Club of Rome EU chapter.

Schops is the recipient of numerous national and international awards and distinctions: 2008 recipient of the Goldman Environmental Prize, better known as the Green Nobel Prize; nominated as an Ashoka fellow as a world-leading social entrepreneur; appointed in 2010 as one of eight global ambassadors for the IUCN, the world's largest environmental network, to support their countdown 2010 initiative to halt the loss of biodiversity. Schops received an honorary doctorate degree from the University of Hasselt in 2011 in recognition of his international work on biodiversity and social entrepreneurship. He became a member of the Climate Leadership Corps of Al Gore in June 2013 and was awarded the title of Commander of the Order of the Crown by King Philippe of Belgium for his services to the state in November 2013.

Ignace Schops is one of the initiators of the 'KLIMAATZAAK' (2014), a climate litigation case against the Belgian Governments for not fulfilling their climate obligations under the Paris Climate Agreement. In 2017, he was selected as one of the 25 most influential Belgians in the world by Charlie Magazine and became a member of the 'Rewilding Circle' of Rewilding Europe. In 2019, the Flemish Parliament awarded him and his organisation the 'Golden Honorary Award' for long-lasting outstanding environmental achievements. In November 2021, Ignace Schops's achievements in the economic sector were acknowledged by the prestigious 'Etion Leadership Award'.

Schops is the author and co-author of several books and articles on herpetology, nature conservation, landscape ecology, social entrepreneurship, sustainable tourism, and other related topics. Belgian bestseller *Gered door de boomkikker (Saved by the Tree Frog)* was originally published in Dutch in 2022. Schops contributed to *Green Growth and Travelism, Letters from Leaders*, for the UN Earth Summit in Rio de Janeiro, 2012.

Ignace Schops is a frequent keynote speaker at international conferences and has presented at Earth Summit Rio +20 – Brazil; World Conservation Congress IUCN (WCC) in Jeju, South Korea; Ashoka Change Nation in Ireland; World Exhibition Shanghai in China; World Nature Summit – Convention on Biological Diversity, Nagoya, Japan; World Congress Ashoka, Paris; and several International Conferences at the EU level.